"Men have forgotten this truth," said the fox.
"But you must not forget it. You become responsible,
forever, for what you have tamed."

—From *The Little Prince*
Antoine de Saint-Exupéry

When Your Pet Outlives You

Protecting Animal Companions After You Die

David Congalton
&
Charlotte Alexander

NewSage Press
Troutdale, Oregon

When Your Pet Outlives You:
Protecting Animal Companions After You Die

Copyright © 2002 Charlotte Alexander and David Congalton
Paperback Original ISBN 0-939165-44-9

NewSage Press
PO Box 607
Troutdale, OR 97060-0607
503-695-2211

website: www.newsagepress.com
email: info@newsagepress.com

Cover Design by George Foster
Book Design by Patricia Keelin
Cover Photos © Sumner Fowler
Photo of Parrot © The Gabriel Foundation

Distributed in the United States and Canada by
Publishers Group West 800-788-3123

Publisher's Cataloging Information

Congalton, David, 1953-
Alexander, Charlotte, 1956-

When Your Pet Outlives You: Protecting Animal Companions After You Die /
David Congalton and Charlotte Alexander

Includes bibliographical references, resources, sample documents for wills, and index.

ISBN 0-939165-44-9 (pbk.)

1.Pet owners—legal protection for their pets. 2. Pet owners—appointing a legal pet caretaker if owner dies. 3.Pets—legal considerations in wills and trusts. 4.Pets—state laws for pets in wills and trusts. 5. Pets—Setting up a pet trust. 6.Pets—Retirement homes for pets. 7.Pets—Sanctuaries for pets. 8. Pets—establishing an I.D. system. 9.Pets—Veterinarians and veterinary schools for legal protection after pet owner's death.

Printed in the United States on recycled paper with soy ink.

1 2 3 4 5 6 7 8 9

For the women of the
North County Humane Society
Atascadero, California

CONTENTS

Acknowledgments

A special debt of gratitude is owed our colleagues from both the Cat Writers Association (CWA) and the Dog Writers Association of America (DWAA) for being so supportive in sharing their stories of pets who outlived their owners. Thanks to Karen Commings, Steve Dale, Deborah Elliott, Lexiann Grant, Dr. Jean Hofve, Karen Lawrence, Lois O'Neill, Sally Spear, Karen Lee Stevens, and Emily Youngreen for embracing this project as if it were their own.

A wonderful pair of Nancys—Nancy Lawson and Nancy Peterson—from The Humane Society of the United States in Washington, D.C. patiently fielded our phone calls and emails and helped develop the national snapshot for our research.

Karen Gray and Anne Cyr gently guided us through the daunting maze of legal research and provided invaluable advice and direction. Vance Hyde edited the early drafts, holding us to a very high standard with her insightful questions and margin notes.

The "Above and Beyond" award this time around goes to our CWA colleague Ginger Buck who moved heaven and earth to track down a radio news story she had heard about an orphaned cat. Thanks, as well, to Sandy Kelley of KTWV 94.7 FM in Los Angeles for not dismissing repeated phone calls from Ginger and retrieving the critical story for us.

The completed manuscript went home to NewSage Press in Troutdale , Oregon where publisher and editor Maureen R. Michelson has treated us like family since our first meeting in 1999. Maureen has never wavered in her support. She knows when to be an editor and when to be a friend. Both are greatly appreciated. And to those whose expertise help bring NewSage Press books to fruition; copy editor Tracy Smith, book designer

Patricia Keelin, cover designer, George Foster, and photographer Sumner Fowler of the Marin Humane Society who captures the uniqueness of each animal he photographs.

Finally, we acknowledge Dr. Cynthia Griffin who first suggested to us that a husband and wife could work together on a major project without the police being called in. Thank you, Dr. Griffin, for the reminder that two are always greater than one.

When Your Pet Outlives You

I Fear Them Losing Me

What happens when your pet outlives you? Consider a few recent examples: In California, a young man died in a tragic boating accident. He left behind a four-year-old dog, a beautiful Queensland mix named Esther. Family and friends discussed what to do with Esther, but nobody wanted her and the young man had left no written instructions. A friend ended up dropping the dog off at the county pound where she spent the next eight days overlooked by people wanting to adopt a younger dog. The day before she was to be euthanized, Esther was adopted by a local dog rescue group.

In Vermont, an elderly farmer died after leaving specific instructions in his will about what should happen to his four horses. Concerned that no one else would be able to match his love and respect for the animals, the farmer instructed that all four horses, considered by state law to be personal property, be put down. A young woman, enraged by the news, organized a statewide campaign to save the horses and challenged the will in court.

In Arizona, a five-year-old Himalayan cat was trapped inside a house for an entire month after her owner suddenly died. No one knew the man had a cat and family members came and went without knowing to look for the animal. By the time the cat was finally discovered and taken to the local humane society, it was too late. The cat died shortly afterwards.

In New York City, visitation was held at a funeral home for an elderly woman who had just died. Her adult grandchildren arrived, carrying the grandmother's two cherished parakeets. Grandma had left no instructions about caring for the birds, leaving others to do what they thought best. The grandchildren couldn't care for the birds properly and had no idea what else to do with them. So right there in front of the casket, the adult grandchildren broke the necks of the two birds and placed their bodies inside the casket next to the grandmother.

$\sim$

Our book is based on the premise that anyone who adopts a dog, a cat, a parrot, a fish, a snake, a horse—any companion animal —does so with a great deal of love and hope and good intentions and just a little bit of nagging fear. That fear is the result of two concerns: (1) Pet owners are afraid that their animals are going to die suddenly and traumatically—hit by a car, attacked by another animal, trapped in a fire, or beset by some type of freak, totally unexpected accident; or (2) pet owners are afraid that *they* are going to die suddenly and traumatically in some type of freak, totally unexpected accident, and that no one will be around to care for their animals. Their pets then will outlive them.

We have experienced the first scenario, and that made us want to be better prepared for the second. On Sunday evening, December 14, 1997, we left our home in San Luis Obispo, California to attend a holiday office party. Three hours later, we returned to find the inside of our house engulfed in smoke and flames. Our three cats,

Triptych, Tripper, and Trio, and our two dogs, Topper and Tess, were dead inside. That horrific night was our introduction to sudden, multiple pet loss, and became the basis for David's award-winning first book, *Three Cats, Two Dogs, One Journey Through Multiple Pet Loss.*

Today, more than four years after the fire, there is a new pack of cats and dogs in our lives. It is fair to say that you can't walk through our house without being in arm's length of at least one of our animals. One of the ways we dealt with the 1997 tragedy was to immerse ourselves in animal rescue work. Charlotte now serves as president of the North County Humane Society in Atascadero. David co-founded Pound Pirates, a small rescue group that plucks dogs and cats out of the county pound and places them in permanent, loving homes.

The work is rewarding, but we plead guilty to often bringing our work home—to stay. Our small house has become a refuge for more than a few pound rescues, animals no one else wanted. We are blessed with great cats like Hannah, the one-eyed wonder, and Catalina who has been blind since birth. Ginger, our little runt dog, suffered extensive burns down her back as a puppy, but you would never know it to see her happily romp with the others today.

Which brings us back to the very real fear of what happens if our pets outlive us. Less than a year after our fire, we were involved in a major accident when our SUV lost control on an interstate highway and flipped several times before sliding into a tree. Fortunately we were able to walk away with only minor injuries. Our friends Jeff and Ann Fairbanks weren't so lucky; they were killed in a horrible head-on collision in November 1995. In June 2001, Ross and Judi Becker, the highly respected editors of *Good Dog!* magazine, both died in an automobile accident. Bad things happen to good people, even good people with pets.

Talking things over, we realized how woefully unprepared

we were in case of an unfortunate accident. True, Charlotte has maintained very detailed medical records on each of our pets, but that was pretty much it. If we died tomorrow, what would happen to our animals? Who would come to our house? How would someone know which pet was which? Where would the animals go to live and who would pay their expenses? How would someone know, for example, that Simon and Ginger are two dogs who are figuratively joined at the hip and shouldn't be separated? How would they know that power-hungry Tiberius needs his daily medication so that he doesn't beat up the other cats? Who would explain about Tanner's sensitive skin condition and the regular treatment he requires? And perhaps the greatest nagging question of all—what steps had we taken to guarantee that if something happened to us, our pets would not end up back on death row at the county pound?

It soon became obvious that others share our concern. A fellow cat-lover from Pennsylvania recently wrote to us about her fear:

> Outliving my cats is the one thing in the world I wish for, even more than winning the lottery. It terrifies me to think that they would be left by themselves. I've given the subject a lot of thought but have not come to any conclusions about what I want to have done. I have no heirs and wouldn't subject them to a friend or my sister. I'm thinking of contacting a local no-kill shelter to ask what amount of money I could leave them if they would take my "kids." Of my twelve, eight are over the age of ten, so hopefully by the time I go, most will have gone too. That's a funny way of looking at it, but more than losing them, I fear them losing me.

Our purpose is neither to provide a detailed legal tome nor a complete estate planning primer, though we certainly address important legal and financial issues regarding how best to provide for your companion animals. What we offer first and foremost is a wake-up call for the average pet owner. There is only so much you can do to keep your animals from being hit by a car or suddenly running off. However, taking the time to work through some important decisions now could allow you to rest in peace about what will happen to your animals after you're gone. Our message is that you need to start planning today.

TWO

Animals in Our Lives

Americans love their pets. The bond between humans and animal companions has never been stronger. According to the American Veterinary Medical Association, more than 58 million American households have at least one companion animal. Here is a breakdown of the U.S. domestic animal population: 59 million cats, 55 million fish, 53 million dogs, 12.6 million birds, 4.8 million rodents, 4 million horses, 3.5 million reptiles.

Animal companions play an increasingly important role in our lives, and study after study, survey after survey, show just how attached and extravagant we have become when pets are involved. In a recent interview published in *The Christian Science Monitor*, Dr. Marty Becker, author of *Chicken Soup for the Pet Lover's Soul*, captured the essence of animals in our lives today. "In our generation," Becker suggests, "pets have made a migration of biblical proportions from the backyard to the bedroom."

More and more, pets are considered part of the family. According to an American Animal Hospital Association (AAHA) survey, 84 percent of pet owners consider their animal companions to be their children. Because they are unable to spend as much time as they would like with their beloved animals, guilt-ridden owners lavish them with gourmet treats and upscale toys. The AAHA survey also found 75 percent of pet owners feel guilty about leaving their pets alone when they go to work, and 74 percent would be willing to go into debt to provide care for their pets. Especially telling is the AAHA finding that over half the respondents said if they were stranded on a deserted island, they would prefer the company of their animal to a human companion!

Pet owners now throw lavish weddings and birthday parties for their dogs and cats. And pets are now an issue in their owners' divorce proceedings. When it comes to our companion animals, we seem to be opening our checkbooks as well as our hearts.

"Pets have become very important in our lives," says Nancy Peterson of The Humane Society of the United States (HSUS). "The bond is really increasing. Animals used to be kept for functions. Dogs had jobs to do, cats did rodent patrol. Today, many of them have the job of being a companion."

According to Peterson, in 1940 less than 8 percent of all U.S. households consisted of people living alone. In the most recent census, however, that number jumped to more than 25 percent. "I think that says a lot about our society," says Peterson. "Many of us live isolated lives. Our family is spread all over the country and sometimes our housemate is a pet. We're spending more quality time with our pets, getting to know them better. When everybody's life is so busy, well, the dog doesn't have an agenda and say, 'Let's see, on Saturday I'm busy so I can't go to the park with you.' No, the dog is there for you, so is the cat, and it's unconditional love. You can't find that anywhere else."

Pets Are Us

A new global study issued in July 2001 by Euro RSCG Worldwide, the world's fifth largest advertising agency network, predicts that annual spending on pets by Americans will soon reach almost $30 billion. The study shows pet pampering on the upswing, concluding, "After centuries of being content with table scraps and a warm corner of the home, pets are now being treated as surrogate children, lavished with premium foods and a wide array of extravagant playthings and accessories."

A growing number of companies also are providing products and services that allow pets to participate in family-oriented activities outside the home. Outdoor adventurers can purchase life preservers, snowshoes, helmets, and other equipment manufactured specifically for dogs.

Dog owners in parts of North America and Europe can attend human-canine summer camps, where owners and their pets spend a week or more together swimming, hiking, playing Frisbee, and having fun in the company of other dogs and their owners. The Animal Legal Defense Fund reports that there are at least thirty-five pet vacation resorts in the United States.

Don Jordan of Seattle Animal Control isn't surprised by all the attention—and money—being lavished on our pets. "We've had a great economy in recent years and people have more disposable income. We've seen more bed and breakfast places for dogs, more dog walking services. People are putting out big bucks, maybe four, five, six hundred dollars a month, to have professionals give personal attention to their animals."

Someone must be reading all those marketing studies about the strength of the human-animal bond. We know, for example, that people are extremely devoted to their pets, often bragging about them to their friends (80 percent), carrying pictures of their pets in their wallets (79 percent), displaying photos around the house of their pets (41 percent) and even taking time off from work to be at home with sick pets (31 percent). Nearly 60 percent of pet owners share their beds with their animals and 20 percent have ended a romantic relationship because the other person involved could not or would not include a pet in their lives.

Pet lovers are generous—almost 80 percent of us admit to giving our pets either a birthday or holiday present. During the December 1999 holiday season pet owners spent an average of $95 on gifts for their pets—28 percent of pet owners spend more on Christmas gifts for their pets than for their spouses. And more than half of pet owners spend more on their animal companions than on their in-laws. All of which led *The Christian Science Monitor* to conclude, "Pets aren't just part of the family. Lately, they've moved to head of the household."

$\sim$

In 1990, a British woman died and left $30,000 to the popular royal corgi dogs of Buckingham Palace.

$\sim$

What are we looking for from our animals? The responses are especially interesting here. Many pet owners claim they gain more friendship and companionship from their pets than from neighbors or friends. A separate survey by the American Pet Association identified the following reasons why Americans have pets: (1) Someone to play with; (2) companionship; (3) help their children learn; (4) someone to communicate with; and (5) security.

Pet ownership also is healthy. The proven benefits of having a pet around include reducing stress and depression, lowering the risk of heart disease, lowering blood pressure, shortening the recovery time after a hospitalization, as well as improving mental attitude and concentration. Longevity and pet ownership are frequently interrelated. For many senior citizens, a pet can be their only family, providing love, affection, and a reason to get up in the morning.

Our connection with animals is so strong that 70 percent of pet owners wouldn't hesitate to spend anywhere between $500 and $5,000 on medical care to avoid euthanizing their pet. As these survey responses underscore, pet owners increasingly see themselves in a parental role, driven by similar emotions of love, guilt, pleasure, and a deep sense of responsibility. But numbers don't tell the whole story of animals in our lives. Consider the story of Wilda, a Norwegian elkhound, and her human companion, Lois.

A Second Chance at Love

Lois O'Neill of Evansville, Indiana said goodbye to her precious dog Thor in August 1999 after his long fight with kidney failure. The beautiful Norwegian elkhound had been with Lois for nearly fifteen years. Her grief was understandably overwhelming, and the last thing she wanted was another dog. But one day Lois visited the National Elkhound Rescue web site, scrolling through the various photographs and case studies. One dog immediately stood out. The description read:

> Wilda, a young seven-year-old female. Former show dog. Owner is recently deceased. Beautiful dog, friendly and loving; gets along with other dogs and cats. Very affectionate to people. Being spayed currently. Available as soon as she recovers.

Her adult children urged Lois to consider adopting a puppy instead of an older dog; they even offered to pay. But Lois didn't want a puppy this time. She was drawn to that photo of Wilda on her computer.

"I have never taken in an older dog," Lois admits. "And because Wilda was so far away, I didn't get a chance to even meet her. 'It was too soon,' I told myself. But, she sounded perfect and I thought that if I didn't take her now, she might not be available.

I called the woman who was fostering Wilda and we had a long talk. I finally said I needed a few days to think things over and asked her to send me a photo. As it turns out, I didn't wait for the photo. The very next day, I called the woman back and said, 'I want Wilda.' The woman wasn't surprised. She knew I'd be calling."

At the time, Wilda was staying just outside Washington, D.C. A few weeks later, she was flown to St. Louis and Lois was waiting. Once at her new home, the dog settled in quickly, sleeping by Lois's bed all night, ignoring the nearby crate Lois had set up. One year later, Lois shared her delight with friends on the Internet:

> Wilda is the only dog that I didn't raise from a puppy. We have bonded so strongly in the last year. I didn't think a bond so close was possible with an older dog. I took a photo of her dressed as a chef and submitted it for a dog-related cookbook about to be published. She was chosen to be on the cover! Wilda is healthy, happy and much loved; this dog is everything I could possibly want. What a joy she is.

An older dog and a woman with a broken heart, both getting a second chance at love. Yes, numbers reflect interesting current trends, but Lois and Wilda are living examples of the endearing nature of the human-animal bond. Animals in our lives, regardless of species or age, are an everlasting and unconditional source of love.

THREE

Why Our Pets Need Protection

Take a moment and consider your own situation. If in the next twenty-four hours you were to die suddenly or wind up in the hospital under extended care, what would happen to your companion animals? To what extent, if any, have you mapped out contingency plans to protect them? They already depend on us for so many things. We make sure they stay healthy, we try to feed our pets properly, and we spend quality time with them. But how many of us have already gone that extra step to make sure our animal companions are safe if something unexpected happens to *us?*

The answer is, not many. Estimates vary, but only about 20 percent of pet owners currently mention their animals in their wills. One study of senior citizens living independently in Chicago revealed that most pet owners just assume that a family member or friend will take care of their pets after an owner's death. Surprisingly, fewer than 2 percent of the pet owners had made any specific legal provisions for funds to support their pets.

Perhaps you have written a will with your animals in mind, but are there instructions to care for your pets before your will is admitted to probate? What steps have you taken to protect your pets in the short term? How about the long term?

Julie Weiss Murad serves as executive director of The Gabriel Foundation, a Colorado-based parrot rescue group. She believes pet owners have an obligation to plan ahead for their pets because the consequences are so high if they don't. "If you don't come home for some reason, someone is eventually going to call animal control. If you haven't left any instructions or directions regarding your pets in your house, animal control is going to come in. They will take your dogs, your cats, and your birds and do with them whatever."

Increased Life Expectancy

The problem is compounded because our pets are living longer. According to Bonnie Wilcox, DVM and Chris Walkowicz in their book *Old Dogs, Old Friends*, "Pets are living longer today. In the past fifty years, their life span has nearly doubled, a cause for rejoicing." A report issued in 2001 by the Purina Pet Institute found that nearly one-third of dog owners and more than one-third of cat owners live with a senior pet, defined as being seven years of age or older.

Indoor cats today regularly live to be 18 or older. It is not unusual for a dog to be blessed with twelve to fifteen good years, or more. Reptiles are increasingly popular pets and typically have a long life expectancy. Certain snakes, for example, can live for twenty years. The California Turtle and Tortoise Club reminds potential owners that turtles may live to be 50 and desert tortoises have been known to live longer than eighty years. One amazing example of longevity is the tortoise Lady. A Nevada woman owned Lady for more than fifty years. When the woman died, in her will she left Lady to her daughter. When the daughter eventually died, her adult children fought over the right to inherit Lady next.

Birds regularly outlive their original owners and may end up with multiple families during their lives. Cockatiels and parakeets can hit the twenty-year mark, and various parrots are still squawking after eighty years. Macaws and cockatoos, both popular pets, typically live fifty to sixty years. Birds outliving an owner is an age-old problem. Before he was inaugurated President of the United States in 1829, Andrew Jackson bought a parrot for his wife. Mrs. Jackson died; the parrot lived on and stayed at the Hermitage in Tennessee, eventually even outliving the President. It is said that the parrot was taken to Jackson's funeral, where the parrot interrupted the ceremony with a loud string of profanity.

It is generally accepted that pets are living longer, and because of various factors, such longevity will only increase in the future. John J. McGonagle of the American Cat Fanciers Association reports that the average life span of a cat increases every year. That's the good news. But with it comes increased responsibility for pet owners, especially those of us who may be older, who may be in poor health, or who tend to live alone.

The staff at the Arizona Humane Society in Phoenix has experienced a variety of difficult rescue situations over the years, but one involving an elderly man and his cat was a particular heartbreaker. Someone showed up at the shelter one day with a dehydrated and emaciated five-year-old Himalayan cat. Normally, a cat like this would be eight to ten pounds. This poor girl weighed in at barely two pounds.

The cat's owner had recently died, the person explained to the horrified staff. She had been left alone in the house for an entire month after the man's death. No one in his family knew the man even had a cat and only discovered her when they were cleaning out the house weeks later; apparently the cat had been hiding all this time. No one in the family wanted a cat who was little more than skin and bones. Staff members tried in vain to save the sickly cat's life, but there was simply too much damage to her internal organs because of the prolonged starvation. She died shortly thereafter.

Dire consequences may await your companion animals if you fail them. Your pets will only be safe if you plan ahead.

Pets and Senior Citizens

All too often, pet owners assume that if something horrible happens to them, surely someone—a family member or friend—will instantly step forward and take care of their pets. They assume that there are others who love their animals as much as they do, people who will make the same emotional commitment. Yes, it's been known to happen, but not often enough.

Instead, what one reporter discovered is perhaps far more typical. Nancy Weaver Teichert documented the plight of orphaned pets in an article written in 2000 for *The Sacramento Bee*. Teichert described how adult children often recoil from the responsibility of taking a parent's pet into their home. After the death of a parent, family members refuse to adopt the pet for any number of reasons. As a result, family, friends, pet rescue organizations, and employees of hospice programs, senior centers and nursing homes are challenged to help place a flood of orphaned pets. The pets often end up being dumped at animal shelters, or in the worst cases, merely abandoned on the street.

According to Sherrie Walker of Animal Allies of Texas, ten to fifteen million pets are abandoned in the United States each year, many of these animals turned out by people (or relatives of people) who have become too ill or simply incapable of caring for them any longer. There was the case in Sacramento of Smokey, a declawed cat with a medical condition who was physically thrown out of the house by an elderly woman's son when it came time for the woman to move into a convalescent home. Neighbors alerted Happy Tails Pet Sanctuary, a local rescue group, and Smokey was eventually placed in a new home. Today, Happy Tails maintains the Smokey Fund, designed to help seniors pay veterinary bills.

Robin Rosner is a senior care specialist based in Cleveland. Rosner is always concerned when she comes across older clients with pets because few have bothered to do any serious planning. "In most cases, I find my clients don't think about the future for their little ones, especially if they have family. They always automatically assume that family will take care of their pets."

Rosner remembers a client, an older woman who had "an adorable little pup." The two were inseparable. Then the woman became critically ill and was hospitalized for an extended period. In the interim, a concerned neighbor volunteered to take care of the dog. The two got along just fine, and when the older woman finally returned home, she quickly realized that the dog really belonged now to her neighbor. In many ways, it was a blessing, according to Rosner, because the older woman needed to move into assisted living, but she had been reluctant because no place would take a dog.

Anxiety among seniors regarding their pets is commonplace; such feelings are only fueled when there is no long-term care established for loyal companions. On the one hand, research has repeatedly shown that seniors who have pets enjoy better health and lifestyle. On the other hand, pet ownership can be a mixed blessing because many of these same seniors worry about what will happen to their animals, and they often delay moving into nursing homes or other extended care facilities out of concern for their pets.

Emily Youngreen works as a home support supervisor in a small British Columbia town, overseeing a staff of fifteen workers who look after the day-to-day care of Canadian senior citizens so that they may remain in their homes as long as possible. As a result, Youngreen has been close to many seniors who have faced difficult decisions about entering extended care facilities.

Martha is one of Youngreen's clients. She is completely housebound and unable to leave her bed—even sitting in her wheelchair has become too painful. Martha has no close family and is dependent on the limited number of hours home support workers can provide with help from church members to fill in the gaps.

Not wanting to be a burden to those who are trying to care for her, Martha would gladly enter an extended care facility—except for Snowflake, a large long-haired black cat who is devoted to her. No area facility will accept a cat, a somber fact that Emily considers tragic. She and her staff have been working on trying to place Snowflake in another home, but that has proven difficult.

Meanwhile, Martha, whom Youngreen describes as "an absolutely lovely lady," suffers at home, filled with anxiety for the fate of her feline companion. Like many of the seniors Youngreen encounters, loneliness is an important issue for Martha. Snowflake has been her antidote.

"With Snowflake around, she has a close relationship with a non-judgmental friend who is always there for her, and needs her," says Youngreen. "Snowflake's freely given affection provides Martha a sense of purpose and self-worth that diminishes her suffering somewhat. And so they stay together. I would hate to think of this dear pet having to spend the rest of her days boarded at the local veterinarian's kennel. She is still so young."

Animal Shelters Are Overwhelmed

More than five thousand animal rescue groups are active in this country alone. Now consider what they are up against. Current statistics from the Society for Improvement of Conditions of Stray Animals (SICSA) show that if every dog or cat in the United States had a home, that would mean that every man, woman, and child in this county would have eight dogs and forty-one cats. More than fifteen million dogs and cats are euthanized in animal shelters across the nation annually. Because most shelters have such a traditional emphasis on dogs and cats, they currently handle less than 1 percent of the nationwide abandoned parrot population.

Given these circumstances, what chance does your companion animal realistically have if he or she ends up being sent to a shelter because there is no alternate plan of action available? The assumption, "Hey, if something happens to me, well, then somebody will take Sam or Cleo over to the shelter and they'll get adopted. I won't worry," flies in the face of reality. Especially if the animal in question is older.

Anyone involved with rescue work with tell you that older animals are always the most difficult to place, and always the first candidates for euthanasia. According to the Zimmer Foundation of Ann Arbor, Michigan, 90 percent of all cats adopted from shelters are kittens. What chance does that give your eleven-year-old tabby? Not much, suggests foundation director Kitty Zimmer. "The older cat will likely be put down because traditional animal shelters find cats over 5 years old difficult if not impossible to place."

Then there's the story of Coco and Alice, the devoted canine companions of an elderly woman living just outside Atlanta. By all accounts, the woman loved her dogs dearly and doted on them at every opportunity. However, she never planned ahead to protect the dogs in the event of her death. When she died in the spring of 2001, her relatives, not knowing what else to do, took Coco and Alice to the local humane society to be euthanized.

Several days later, and just before the scheduled euthanizing, Coco and Alice were adopted by a rescue group specializing in senior dogs. Unfortunately, the damage had been done. Alice succumbed to a stroke and cardiac arrest, brought on by what rescue officials called the stress of displacement and life at the shelter. Coco, a seven-year-old purebred cocker spaniel, was suddenly left on her own.

Is there an animal organization in the country right now that couldn't use more space, more money, more volunteers, more supplies—and fewer animals? The last thing they need is an apathetic family member assuming that rescue groups will readily step in and care for orphaned pets.

"There's a lot of chaos following someone's death and it definitely affects the animals," says Diane Allevato, executive director of the Marin Humane Society in Novato, California. "People are coming and going out of the house and the cats get freaked out, so they split. Or dinner isn't served promptly. Gates get left open so a dog gets out and is hit by a car. A lot of these stories happen relatively routinely—animals being lost, killed, or given up. It's especially tragic because these were beloved companions."

~

Very few pets will live their entire lives with the same family. The national retention rate for an adopted pet's stay in the adopter's home after the first year is less than 35 percent, according to the Society for Improvement of Conditions of Stray Animals (SICSA). Many are returned to the shelter, given away, dumped in the country, or left to wander.

~

Parrots: A Special Challenge

Three to five million parrots live in the United States. About 30 percent are living in less than desirable conditions. According to The Gabriel Foundation, the average parrot can have up to fourteen different owners in his or her lifetime. Many parrots will have been in three different homes by the age of 5. Compounding the problem, birds live an incredibly long time, some upwards of eighty years. The median age for a parrot is 45, making them particularly vulnerable to outliving their owners and a special challenge for anyone who adopts them.

Parrots can be loud, they can bite, they can be messier than a roomful of teen-agers. Adding to the challenge is the nearly 30 percent increase in parrot ownership just in the last decade.

Unfortunately, the number of homeless parrots also is increasing.

If an owner dies, people who step in to help care for the parrot face limited options. It is not uncommon for birds to end up being passed from home to home. "What's quite common is for someone to keep a bird thirty, forty, even fifty years. They become quite attached to one another," says Julie Weiss Murad of the Gabriel Foundation. "Then the human dies and the family doesn't want to deal with the bird. They just can't handle it. We see it all too frequently."

Those parrots lucky enough to end up in a pet sanctuary like The Gabriel Foundation typically have gone through three to six homes first. Some people try contacting zoos to see if they will accept a bird. The Bronx Zoo gets dozens of phone calls daily from people hoping it will take unwanted birds, but that is seldom an option unless the breed is especially rare.

Many parrots end up for sale on consignment at the local pet store because the surviving family members can't handle them. Or they're just dumped, let loose to fend for themselves. Horror stories abound of parrots burned with cigarettes, left in freezing conditions, or abandoned in basements to die by people who don't know how to care for them properly, or who simply abuse them.

Helen Fahlsing rescues birds through Charlie's Bird House in Gatesville, Texas. Many of the birds she takes in are survivors of their original owners. Most end up in garages or sheds because the other members of the family did not like or want the bird in the first place.

Fahlsing faces almost daily heartbreak when she sees how some birds end up being treated. "You have to wonder how many companion bird owners have thought about what will happen when they die," she says. "Who's going to take care of the bird? Where's it going to end up? In someone's home being cared for, but not loved, or at some auction along with other exotics? Or just abandoned? I've got news for them—the zoos and regular shelters aren't equipped to take birds, and most of their relatives probably don't like or want the bird."

Working part-time as a home health nurse in Texas, Fahlsing says it is a particular problem for her elderly patients. Many patients do not have any family in the immediate area so they depend on pets for some small degree of companionship. Yet these people have not bothered to tell neighbors about their inside pets in case something happens.

One of Fahlsing's clients was an elderly woman who lapsed into unconsciousness and was hospitalized for an extended time. Thoughtful neighbors kept an eye on the dog in the back yard, providing food and water daily. But no one knew that the woman also had three parakeets inside the house. When the woman regained consciousness and returned home, it was too late. The birds were dead.

The Pets JFK, Jr. Left Behind

John F. Kennedy, Jr., his wife Carolyn Bessette, and her sister Lauren Bessette died on July 16, 1999 when their airplane plunged into the Atlantic Ocean off the coast of Martha's Vineyard. The world was stunned to learn of their tragic deaths.

Anxiety rippled through the dog world as well, because anyone who saw the tabloid photos of Kennedy and Bessette in recent years could not miss Friday, their family dog. Press accounts always mistakenly referred to Friday as a "shelter rescue," when in fact he was a rare, purebred Canaan dog.

Friday was a constant companion to the pop icon couple, helping them fight off the *paparazzi* as they wandered Manhattan. One evening, a photographer started to pet Friday who was tied up outside a Manhattan diner. Kennedy supposedly stormed out to the curb and yelled, "If you guys are going to be inhumane to my wife, you shouldn't pet my dog."

So with news of the plane crash, there was concern that Friday was also on board. Thankfully, he stayed home that weekend with Ruby, their adopted black feline who accompanied Bessette into her marriage.

Details of Kennedy's will, running three-and-a-half pages, were announced the following September, singling out family, friends, and favorite charities as prime beneficiaries. Mentioned in the will, for example, were Kennedy's North Moore Street co-op in Manhattan, as well as real estate co-owned by Kennedy and his sister, Caroline Kennedy Schlossberg. Kennedy made a point of mentioning specific people, including several family members, a nanny, a former butler, two godchildren, a longtime administrative assistant at *George* magazine, and the John F. Kennedy Library and Museum in Boston.

However, one detail was missing—no mention of either Friday or Ruby in the will. Kennedy failed to make the necessary provisions for two pets whom he and his wife clearly cherished.

Several press accounts detail the care and attention Kennedy devoted to selecting and purchasing Friday from an Illinois breeder in 1995. Yet, for some reason, Kennedy never got around to demonstrating that same care and attention for his companion animals when it came to his estate planning. In this case, the vast Kennedy fortune afforded a safety net that most pet owners do not have. A family caretaker who had spent considerable time with both Ruby and Friday took the animals temporarily while there was talk of both animals eventually going to live with sister Caroline.

The Kennedy-Bessette tragedy reminds us that no one with pets—no one—is immune from the issues we raise. Dying before your pets die is not a concern merely for the elderly. People die far too young every hour of every day and many of them have pets who need to be protected. Ruby and Friday will be just fine, but they're the exceptions.

Celebrities and Their Pets

In contrast to the Kennedy-Bessette case, consider what some famous celebrities have done to protect their pets over the years. Tobacco heiress Doris Duke left $100,000 in trust for the benefit of her dog, Minni. Natalie Schafer, the actress who portrayed Mrs. Howell on TV's "Gilligan's Island," provided that her fortune be used for the benefit of her dog. Actress Betty White has a will that leaves her reported $5 million estate literally to the dogs, while Oprah Winfrey has already taken steps to make sure her dogs live out their lives in luxury.

The late British singer Dusty Springfield included extensive provisions in her will for her cat, Nicholas. Her will instructed that the cat's bed be lined with Springfield's nightgown, that the singer's recordings be played each night at his bedtime, and that Nicholas be fed imported baby food.

Then there's the case of Malcolm, the fourteen-year-old black pug who belonged to actress Sylvia Sidney. When Sidney, who appeared in more than sixty films over the course of six decades, died in 1999 at the age of 88, she had no friends or living relatives who could adopt Malcolm.

Fortunately, she had made arrangements for Malcolm to move into the lavish National Arts Club in the Samuel Tilden mansion in New York City. What a life! Malcolm is walked five times daily and visits a veterinarian every two weeks. One year he even hosted a party for out-of-town dogs attending the Westminster Kennel Club Show at Madison Square Garden.

Most of us don't have the lavish resources to provide for our pets in a similar fashion, but that's not the point. In each of these cases, these pet owners recognized the need to do something to protect their animals. They understood that if something wasn't done now, their animals would be placed at risk later.

Do Not Depend on Verbal Agreements

It happens far too often. People who for one reason or another must give up their pets put them up for adoption without being careful about who ends up with them. Often so relieved to find someone, anyone, willing to take an older cat or a squawking parrot or a stubborn basset hound, they let someone "who seems so nice" take their animals without getting anything in writing, assuming that everything will be fine.

We have a friend who does periodic animal rescue work. When she arranges the adoption of a cat or a dog to a prospective family, not only does she do a home visit, but the adopters are required to sign a two-page contract spelling out the terms of endearment. "There are too many strange people out there," she explains. "I've learned to get everything in writing."

Kimberly and Neale Cox learned this lesson the hard way. According to a *Seattle Times* report, they lived just north of Seattle in the small, rustic hamlet of Lake Stevens with their three pet goats—Buster, Oreo, and Martin—and their beloved horse, a twenty-three-year-old strawberry roan named Jubilee. The Coxes loved their animals, but the goats kept escaping from their yard, so Kimberly reluctantly placed an ad in the newspaper: "Free goats to a good home."

A young man responded to the ad, promising to love the goats and provide a great life for them on his acreage. He must have been pretty persuasive; not only did he get Buster, Oreo, and Martin, he also ended up with Jubilee. The Coxes originally weren't looking to place the horse, but they felt sorry for their elderly horse being so alone without the goats and relented after the young man allegedly talked up his own two horses and how the Coxes could come visit weekly.

Remember the old saying about what happens when something sounds too good to be true? The Coxes surrendered their animals without the protection of a written contract, and the young man took the three goats and Jubilee home.

Then he turned around and sold all four animals for slaughter, making a profit of $864.

Buster, Oreo, and Martin ended up on the block at a livestock auction, while old Jubilee was shipped to a Canadian company that sells horse meat to Europe for human consumption.

The Coxes learned the shocking news when they later tried to check up on the animals. A public outcry ensued. However, no laws were broken. Law enforcement officials claimed a lack the evidence for criminal charges, but the Coxes plan to sue the young man for contract fraud and the tort of outrage, which involves a significant infliction of emotional stress.

The young man claims he had to sell off the animals. The goats were escaping from his yard and Jubilee's feet were in terrible condition; he was just trying to do the humane thing. That was before the Seattle media interviewed a spokesperson for the Marysville Livestock Auction who described the young man as a regular customer who brought in goats and sheep for sale at least once a month. "Maybe that's what people should know," the auction spokesperson said. "There's no such thing as 'free to a good home' when you advertise in the paper."

The Coxes learned an important lesson about the weakness of verbal agreements. You might shake your head at this story and think, "They shouldn't have placed that newspaper ad. What were they thinking in trusting a complete stranger?" Now what about the person who makes a verbal agreement with a local humane society, an established and respected shelter with a history of good work? Would a verbal agreement with such a shelter be enough?

Bonnie thought so. She was a woman who lived alone in a small Central California town. First diagnosed with cancer in early 2000, Bonnie knew the clock was running out. She had already made arrangements to spend her final months with her daughter, who lived out of state. She was at peace with what was about to happen. At this point, there was only one thing that really mattered to Bonnie.

Actually, there were sixteen things; that's how many cats Bonnie kept in her house, and in her heart. The cat pack included Smudge, the very affectionate Russian Blue, and Angel, the lap kitty calico who liked to give gentle nips. Blackie, the aptly named solid black cat, loved to go for walks, while another black male, Spooky, was shy but loving. Cinder, a seven-year-old brown tabby female, talked a lot and enjoyed sitting next to people, and Tabitha, the Maine coon, was known for her nip kisses. Girlie, the silver tabby, acted like a natural lover, and another calico named Misty was just plain sweet. Mitzer always demanded attention and Tommy Boy constantly sped throughout the house like a cyclone of fur.

These cats, along with the others, meant the world to Bonnie. She wanted to make sure that her feline family was well cared for. She decided to contact a local humane society and explain her situation.

"I have about a year left before I move out of state," Bonnie told the shelter. "Obviously, I can't take the cats with me, but I want them to stay with me as long as I'm healthy and able to care for them. When it's time, will you please take my cats and find them good, loving homes?"

The humane society agreed to assist Bonnie, who in turn would make a donation to help cover shelter expenses. Nothing was put in writing. At that point, it didn't seem necessary.

Months passed and Bonnie's health continually declined. Along the way, she added a litter of four rescue kittens to the mix—a female Russian Blue, a male tabby and two gray-and-white female tabby kittens. Even the shadow of death couldn't keep Bonnie from her rescue work. Now there were twenty cats in her house.

Bonnie told friends that she would know when it would be time to say goodbye to her beloved cats. The moment finally came one April morning when Bonnie called the humane society. Tearfully, she asked them to come out and take her cats away. Weak from the cancer and able to move only with great difficulty, Bonnie wrestled with a constant shortness of breath. Friends had to help feed her cats and clean the litter boxes. Meanwhile, Bonnie's concerned daughter kept urging Bonnie to make the move. Through it all, the one constant source of comfort was her cats and the relief in knowing they would be cared for.

But Bonnie, who at this stage of her life thought there were no surprises left, received disturbing news. Humane society staff members apologetically explained that they would be unable to help her as originally promised. This was kitten season, after all, and the cramped shelter was already overwhelmed. The humane society was short on space, foster homes, and volunteers. It would be impossible to accept any of her cats, not even one, not even the kittens.

Bonnie was anguished at the news; she simply did not know what to do. For the last year, she had been counting on the shelter, and now, suddenly, the staff had changed their minds. Even worse, Bonnie didn't have a backup plan. She didn't think she needed one. Bonnie had already made arrangements to leave town, but cancer or no cancer, she had to do something to protect her companion animals.

Friends began contacting local cat rescue groups. "Please help! We have to find good homes for twenty cats and kittens before May 7th. Those that don't find homes will have to be turned into the pound. Please help. Please." Rescue groups posted phone numbers and exchanged ideas. Five of the cats were adopted right away, and a sixth was placed in a foster home—fourteen to go.

Stories about people dying of cancer are not expected to have happy endings, but there is some good news to report about Bonnie's menagerie. The rescue groups came through for her—all twenty cats and kittens ended up safe in permanent or temporary foster homes before she had to move. Bonnie was greatly comforted as she left town to be with her daughter.

Like the Coxes in Seattle, Bonnie thought she was doing the right thing in giving her animals away, but what happened in both of these cases is a painful reminder that good intentions are not enough. When your pets are involved, the days of a simple handshake and friendly smile are long gone. Verbal agreements can lead to misunderstanding, confusion, and needless endangerment of animals.

If you are opting to give up any of your pets, for any reason, you must make sure those pets will be safe in their new environment. And you must get everything in writing. For all these reasons, and many more, pets need our protection. We like the advice Helen Fahlsing from Charlie's Bird House in Texas offers. "Just remember, when you sit down to make arrangements for the kids, the house, the car—don't forget the dog, the cat, and the bird."

FOUR

Establishing a Pet ID System

Betty was a physical therapist in Colorado whose specialty was working with disabled children. Betty loved her job as much as she loved her animals. There were nine in all: two horses, one cat, one canary, one cockatiel, two parrots, and two wolves. The wolves had their own three-acre enclosed space. Having all these animals made Betty, who lived alone in a rural area, quite happy. She divided her time between her two passions—children and animals.

One day Betty, who was only 46, was sitting in her truck outside the grocery store. She had a heart attack and died. No passersby noticed the body for two days and by the time anyone could get out to Betty's house, three full days had passed.

All of Betty's animals were safe, but no one could find any paperwork or medical records in the house, except for documents indicating that the two parrots had been adopted from the Gabriel Foundation sanctuary in Aspen, Colorado. The two parrots were returned to the foundation. The other seven animals were euthanized. "This is not what she would have wanted," says Julie Weiss Murad, executive director of The Gabriel Foundation.

The Question of Pet Identification

Think about your pets, and your house. What do you know about your animals and how much of that information is fully documented? Try to imagine a scenario where you have suddenly, unexpectedly, died, but your two cats, one dog, and parrot are very much alive and at home, probably hungry and waiting anxiously for your return. Instead of you, now a close friend or concerned neighbor walks through your front door to care for your animal companions—assuming, of course, that you have left a key with someone in case of emergencies.

Maybe you are not even dead, but you have been in a serious car accident or fall, and won't be home for days. Try to picture family and friends in your home, anxiously looking for any kind of records or helpful information about your animals. What would they find? How hard would it be for them to locate everything? Have you taken the time to assemble and organize all the important paperwork and emergency care information about your pets? And have you made it easy enough to find?

The answer is probably no. You are not alone. Most caring pet owners have not thought through any contingency plan for their animal companions. However, establishing some type of overall pet identification system is paramount for emergency situations. Nina Berkheiser of the SPCA of Pinellas County in Florida is always counseling pet owners to be prepared in case there is a medical emergency. "If you have a heart attack and the EMTs show up, they don't know what to with these pets. If somebody doesn't know what to do and you're in the hospital for three days, then these animals aren't going to be in real good shape."

Twenty-One Orphaned Cats

On January 5, 1998, well-known cat breeder Erma Jenei and her son David were killed instantly in a car/truck collision in eastern Ontario. They were the first victims of a dreadful ice storm that ravaged northeastern Canada that winter. David had been married for only four months.

Erma, who was a longtime breeder of orientals and Siamese, lived alone in Toronto with her twenty-one cats. Other than David's widow, there was no other family. Friends of David, however, knew about Erma's involvement in the Cat Fanciers' Association (CFA) and began contacting nearby CFA members, including Karen Lawrence. What do we do with all these cats, the friends wanted to know. Karen will never forget the week (and months) that followed.

"My first thought after getting that phone call, besides getting over the shock, was arranging for immediate care of the cats. I called Pam Nichols, a fellow breeder in Toronto and she and a friend, Joanne McKinnon, went out to Erma's house to feed and clean the cats that night. One major concern was how to get into the locked house without raising the curiosity of the neighbors. As luck would have it, Joanne had been a cat sitter for Erma and knew how to get into the house through the garage.

"There were twenty-one cats total waiting, several stashed in cages in a bedroom 'cattery,' including one female with a litter of very young kittens. Others were housed in the bathrooms and several had the run of the house. Fortunately, all the cats were friendly and not afraid of strangers. Pam and Joanne counted the cats, fed them and cleaned the litter pans; leaving behind enough food and water for the next several days.

"On Tuesday, Pam and I discussed what to do next. Our major concern was that the neighbors, who at this point still didn't know about Erma's death, would report the cats to the humane society once they found out their owner had died. We weren't familiar with whether or not the neighbors even knew that Erma bred cats, or if they knew just how many cats she had. However, we knew for certain that Erma would not have wanted the cats surrendered to, or taken by, the humane society. And, adding to the problem, Pam reported the faint smell of gas in the house.

"Fortunately, Erma, who was often away on weekends at cat shows, had left instructions for her cat sitter. Stapled to the wall outside each room that had cats in it was a list of the cats in the room, and for the cattery bedroom, there was even a drawing of the cages in the room and the names of the cats in those cages. Discussion with other breeders who knew Erma's cats confirmed identities. Thus we were able to identify all but the two adult males that were together in one bathroom.

"On Wednesday, the gas company arrived and promptly shut down the furnace because of a gas leak. As it was in the middle of a cold Canadian winter, we had to make a decision about what to do with the twenty-one cats because of the lack of heat. Our only choice was to remove them from the house. We were also very concerned because the neighbors were getting curious about the strange people coming and going from Erma's house and they started to knock on the door and ask questions.

"With permission of the estate, we searched the house for registration paperwork. Finding it was a chore because none of it was in a single file or file drawer. We eventually found various registration certificates and health records, with complete matching paperwork available for only six cats. With the approval and signature of the estate, the ownership on the registration papers was transferred to the new owners of those cats about six months after the accident.

"Erma's house was finally empty of cats, but now I had nine felines living in my laundry room—this was almost double my cat population. The majority of cats, including the litter of kittens, were neutered/spayed and placed in homes over the next few months. Several breeders in the area contributed to our veterinary expenses and the cats were eventually placed in homes for the cost of the spay/neuter. Food and litter costs were borne by the individual breeder fostering the cats. It was a good six months before my laundry room was catless again."

Erma Jenei was fortunate to have such loyal and determined friends who could step in and help rescue her cats. Leaving critical information about her cats made the job of the rescuers easier. However, not having complete documentation presented challenges.

Developing a comprehensive pet ID system is the first major task you need to undertake, whether you have two pets or twenty. Put yourself into a friend or family member's shoes. They have come to your house to care for your pets. What exactly do they need to know? Here is how you tell them.

~

A British pet sanctuary faces an uphill fight in trying to find a new home for two African Greys because the parrots "swear and pass wind." The trouble started when Sydney started teaching Claud the swear words he'd learned in a previous home. According to sanctuary director Julie Pearcey. "They are just terrible and they always pick their moment—normally when I am speaking to someone on the phone."

~

Bring Out the Camera

Begin by recording your animals with a video camera. As you record, provide some type of running monologue describing each pet in detail and any particular idiosyncrasies people might need to know. For instance, "This is Dodger. He's a very friendly dog, but sometimes he's too aggressive with a tennis ball. Be careful if you try to take one away from him. Always speak softly to him first," or "This is our cat, Mortimer. He has to take a pill every morning. Notice how we hold him just so in order to get that pill down his throat. Good luck!" When the tape is completed, label it clearly and keep in an accessible place.

Also, use a still camera to snap photos of each pet. Again, clearly label each photo on the back with the pet's name, approximate age, and date of birth.

Set Up a Pet File System

This is the age of computers, yes, but not everyone knows how to access your computer system and your files. The goal is to make it easy for others to gather emergency information about your pets. Use the computer for your personal records, but keep hard copies of documents available where they can be discovered during even a casual search.

Assign every pet in the house an individual file folder. When someone opens up the folder, the first thing he or she should find is your pet's photo. Information in your pet file system needs to be updated constantly (see Pet File System Checklist on page 39). And remember, all this concentrated effort goes to waste if no one can find it. Place the file, along with the pet videotape, in some prominent spot in your bedroom or home office. Some have suggested putting a note on that ever-popular "house billboard," the kitchen refrigerator, to let people know where they can find the files.

~

In ancient Egypt, when someone died, it was customary for favorite pets to be euthanized and buried with their owner.

~

Prepare a Pet Card

Congratulations, you have your pets videotaped and photographed, and there's a detailed, organized information system established somewhere in your home. But you're not done yet. The next step involves the preparation of a pet card, a small piece of valuable information that can be carried around in your wallet or purse. No two pet cards are going to be the same, but it's quite common for people to list the number of pets they have at home, while also listing one or two phone numbers of friends who can be contacted about emergency pet care (see Sample Pet Card below). If you are killed or injured, emergency personnel will know from your pet card whom to contact to help your animals.

Attorney Mary Randolph, author of the book *Dog Law*, put into perspective the need to carry a pet card when she was interviewed by writer Gina Spadafori. "Your pets may be alone for who knows how long," she said. "Maybe your neighbors don't know where you are, maybe your family lives far away. And if you die and you haven't lined up care, your pets may end up in the shelter after they're found.

Sample Pet Card

If I am unable to return home to care for my ___(#)___ pets because of death or hospitalization, please immediately contact:

_____ at _____
      (NAME)   (ADDRESS/PHONE)

or

_____ at _____
      (NAME)   (ADDRESS/PHONE)

to arrange for care of my pets located at:

_____   _____
     (YOUR ADDRESS)   (PHONE)

Emergency Pet Identification

The Humane Society of the United States (HSUS) has published a free brochure, "Planning for Your Pet's Future Without You." The HSUS suggestions for maintaining an accurate system of emergency pet identification include:

• Find at least two responsible friends or relatives who agree to serve as temporary emergency caregivers in the event that something unexpected happens to you. Provide them with the keys to your home, feeding and care instructions, the name of your veterinarian, and information about the permanent care provisions you have made for your pet.

• Make sure your neighbors, friends, and relatives know how many pets you have and the names and contact numbers of the individuals who have agreed to serve as emergency caregivers. Emergency caregivers should also know how to contact each other.

• Carry a wallet "alert card" (pet card) that lists the names and phone numbers of your emergency pet caregivers.

• Post removable "in case of emergency" notices on your doors or windows specifying how many and what types of pets you have. These notices will alert emergency-response personnel during a fire or other home emergency. Don't use stickers; hard-to-remove stickers are often left behind by former residents, so firefighters may assume that the sticker is outdated or, worse, risk their lives trying to find a pet no longer in the house.

• Affix to the inside of your front and back doors a removable notice listing emergency contact names and phone numbers.

Nancy Peterson of HSUS notes, "As pets have become more a part of the family, people are naturally more concerned about their welfare. Unfortunately, people don't often think about the scenario where they themselves might pass on before their pets, so we're trying to get them to start thinking. Anyone who has pets and cares about them will sleep better at night knowing their pets will be cared for should something happen to them."

Pet File System Checklist

Information that should be included for all your pets:

- Emergency phone numbers and names of veterinarians, pet sitters and boarding kennels.

- Contact information for friends or neighbors who could be called to help with your companion animals.

- Are any of the pets being kept in cages or crates in the house? If so, why? Are there special instructions?

- Recent photo.

- Information about the animal's sex, age, weight, and pedigree.

- A complete pet vaccination record.

- All other relevant medical records, including whether the pet has been spayed or neutered.

- Is the pet pregnant or receiving medication?

- Does the pet have a microchip?

- Are there any distinguishing marks on the pet? Sometimes a photo isn't enough. (We have two cats from the same litter who look identical. The only way a stranger could tell them apart is that Alexander wears a blue collar and Romeo wears a red collar.)

- What type of food does the pet eat? How often?

- Is the pet registered, either with a particular breed organization, or licensed through either the city or the county?

- Are there important social or behavior issues to note? For instance, Bob Barker is afraid of the vacuum cleaner.

FIVE

Appointing a Pet Caretaker

In Chapter Four, we discuss the establishment of a pet identification system to help friends, relatives or neighbors who come forward in an emergency situation to care for your pets.

It is comforting to know such people are around and available at a moment's notice, but you also need to take a much longer view. If something were to happen to you, who would you want to take your pets for the next five, ten, fifteen, or twenty years? Your neighbors might be glad to come over for a week and feed your cats, but perhaps they already have four or five of their own. They certainly can't be expected to let your gang move in permanently.

You also need to ensure that your wishes regarding your animal companions are carried out. Consider the case of an elderly San Diego couple who loved their two parrots. They wanted to know more about proper care and feeding of their birds so the couple began attending free seminars offered by a local parrot rescue and education organization. They never missed a meeting and always sat in the front row.

After the first year, the couple appeared in class less and less frequently. Then one day the organization's executive director received a phone call from the wife, who had been diagnosed with lung cancer. Her husband's health also was declining due to Alzheimer's, so the couple wanted the rescue group to take their two parrots when the time came. The executive director agreed.

However, the wife's health deteriorated faster than expected and nothing was ever formalized. Shortly thereafter, the executive director received a phone call from the woman's daughter. The wife had died that morning and the family was already making arrangements to place the husband in a home. The daughter was calling to see if the executive director could come and clip the birds' wings so that they could be sold through a newspaper ad.

The daughter admitted knowing about her mother's request that both parrots go to the rescue group, but the family members had decided otherwise. The parrots were so expensive, the family reasoned; they needed to sell them and recoup the money in order to pay for the funeral.

The elderly couple had not wanted their beloved parrots to be sold and incorrectly assumed that family members would honor their wishes. Is there anything the couple could have done to protect their parrots in advance?

Yes, you need a pet caretaker, someone whom you trust beyond words, a person you feel will be responsible enough to care for your companion animals should something unfortunate happen to you. That makes the selection of a caretaker one of the most important decisions you will make regarding the future well-being of your animals. While researching on the Internet for this book we found an interesting comment posted on a message board about an agreement two friends made in case one of them died before their animal companions. The message read in part, "My best friend and I each have horses. I dearly love her trusty old fox hunter, so in her will, 'John the horse' is left to me. However, in addition to John, I had to agree to take 'Higgins, the extremely obnoxious parrot.'"

~

An attorney in Arizona was charged with personally benefiting from his role as manager of an estate left to benefit a much-loved dog. In his defense, the attorney argued that the dog enjoyed and could clearly afford riding in a luxury car.

~

Leaving Money for the Dog

There once was a woman named Mrs. Brown, who owned a beautiful black Labrador named Clancy. As she advanced in years, Mrs. Brown became concerned that Clancy would outlive her; she wanted to make sure the dog would be happy and comfortable for the rest of his days. Her estate planner outlined several options, but Mrs. Brown dismissed them all. When Mrs. Brown died, she insisted, Clancy must continue to live in her home.

For this plan to work, someone had to be willing to live in her house and dog sit Clancy until he died. The sixty-four-year-old widower who lived next door agreed to Mrs. Brown's terms: a free place to live, plus $1,200 per month as salary.

The will was set up accordingly: When Mrs. Brown died, the trust department of her local bank would control her cash assets for the rest of Clancy's life. From these assets, the bank trustee would pay the neighbor his monthly salary. Also, the trust department agreed to send someone out twice a year to check on Clancy and make sure the dog was still alive. Once Clancy died, according to the will, the bank would stop the salary, sell the home, and deliver the proceeds and other assets to several pet charities.

Clancy was nine years old when Mrs. Brown died. About a

year later, the bank trustee assigned to Mrs. Brown's estate left the bank and the work was assigned to a new trust officer. As called for in the will, twice-yearly visits were made to check on the dog and the neighbor received his monthly stipend. This pattern repeated itself over the years with various trust officers coming and going; during a twelve-year period, six different staff people were involved. But the neighbor kept receiving his money and Clancy seemed to have turned into a canine Jack LaLane.

Do the math. A dog who was nine when his owner died is still alive twelve years later and bouncing around at the age of 21? Actually, it turns out that Clancy died of natural causes at the age of 14, but the neighbor didn't bother to tell anyone. Instead, he bought another black Labrador and named him Clancy. When that dog died, a third Clancy appeared—and the neighbor continued to get his stipend, plus a free place to live.

Selecting a Pet Caretaker

A pet caretaker is needed because the law does not allow you to leave money directly to animal companions, a judicial doctrine we explore more fully in Chapter Six. Legally, you can leave money only to other "persons," so an animal, by law, cannot do anything with a money bequest without the assistance of a "person."

The good news is that the concept of a pet caretaker is evolving rapidly as more legal options are created. Pet owners increasingly are recognizing the need to plan for either an individual or organization to assume a caretaking role. As we discuss in other chapters, that, in turn, has spawned a wave of new alternatives, including retirement homes for pets, planned giving to humane societies and veterinary schools, plus an impressive rise in the number of states legalizing pet trusts. Despite the richness of options, however, our own sense is that the average pet owner today is most likely to designate a single individual as caretaker.

We also recognize that there are many devoted animal lovers

who don't need a will or any legal mumbo-jumbo to spell out what to do should something unfortunate befall a human friend or loved one. We know that some people would automatically step in, assume responsibility for a loved one's pets, and care for them forever. That's wonderful, but it is still a good idea for pet owners to put affairs of the heart in writing, just in case there is confusion later on. So how do you designate a pet caretaker? The following information offers some basic guidelines.

Find a Good Candidate

All this comes down to one basic question: "Whom do you trust?" There is nothing legally binding in a caretaker arrangement. You are turning your animal companions over to someone, and by law, the pets now become their property; they can do with those animals as they wish. The best you can do is "request" that the caretaker provide your pets a certain level of care. That is why choosing a trustworthy individual is so important.

Gerald Condon and Jeffrey Condon, co-authors of *Beyond the Grave: The Right Way and the Wrong Way to Leave Money to Your Children (and Others)*, devised an interesting formula a few years back: **Caretaker = Compatibility plus Capability.** You want someone whose lifestyle is compatible with that of your pets. If your cats are indoor cats, for example, you don't want them going with someone who will let them outside. If your dog is used to regular companionship, do not put him in a home where he'll be alone much of the time.

There is also the issue of capability. Your neighbors may be swell people, but are they able to handle your loud, messy parrot or two aggressive dogs? The road to the animal pound, unfortunately, is paved with good intentions. People often step forward and agree to take in animals, only to find later they can't handle it. It is crucial that you fully explain your expectations in advance so that there is no doubt about what will happen to your pets when you die.

We suggest a third "C" for your consideration: compassion. You can sense a true pet lover, a devoted animal person, by the way he or she behaves around your animals. Compatibility and capability are necessary in a caretaker, but you should also feel the love in the room when your prospective caretaker is with your pets. If you don't sense that bond immediately, find another person.

Therefore, **Caretaker = Compatibility plus Capability plus Compassion.**

Introduce Your Pets

Ideally, the first time your caretaker meets your pets should not be after you are gone. The more time everyone can spend together now, the easier the transition will be for all concerned later. We are not suggesting that the caretaker become a house guest. Yet there are obvious advantages to letting the caretaker observe how you and your animals interact and what daily routines you follow together. At the same time, the caretaker's presence allows him or her to bond with your pets. That makes it so much easier for the caretaker when it becomes necessary to relocate the animals. The more time all of you can spend together, the better.

Prepare Your Pet Caretaker

The same principle we discussed about preparing pet documents for emergency use applies to working with a long-term caretaker, except now you have an opportunity for one-on-one interaction. What is it that you want known about your pet? What does the caretaker need to know in order to assure that Tristan or Charlie is set for life?

Spend whatever time you feel is needed to prepare your pet caretaker—it will be too late once you are gone. He or she will need to know everything related to medical histories, personalities and habits—yet another argument in favor of maintaining an up-to-date pet identification system. Putting background information on paper is always an excellent idea.

Mention the Pet Caretaker in Your Will

Even if your pet caretaker ends up being a close friend or family member, put everything in writing. Remember, all you are doing is requesting what you would like to have happen with your companion animals. But if you include it in your will, you are underscoring the seriousness of the commitment and you are reminding the caretaker of your wishes, expectations, and gratitude.

The simplest method is to leave your pet or pets to your appointed caretaker in your will with a short mention. For example:

> As we agreed to prior to my death, I leave my two dogs Molly and Tanner, plus my cat Mr. Maxwell, to my neighbor and friend, Mr. Joseph Hill of 1232 Elm Street, together with the sum of $10,000, said funds to be used to defray the costs of the care of Molly, Tanner, and Mr. Maxwell for the remainder of their lives. Should any funds be left over after all three pets have died, Joseph may retain them as an expression of my gratitude for his considerate support.

You could take an extra step and specify your expectations concerning issues such as medical care and grooming, but at this stage, it probably won't matter. If you have chosen the right person, he or she will already have that information from you. And if the caretaker needs to be reminded at this point about how to care properly for a pet, well, this is clearly the wrong person for the job.

Provide Enough Money

There are those rare individuals who will gladly step forward and lovingly care for your animals should something happen to you. There are others, however, who will gladly step forward and lovingly care for your animals—but the household budget is tight and we all know how expensive feeding pets can be.

The issue of money should be clearly discussed up front with your caretaker, because you do not want your animals to become a financial burden on someone else. Consider legitimate pet expenses, including food, routine veterinary care, boarding costs, and other expenses in deciding how much money to leave. A discussion with your caretaker should include:

• How much money can you afford to leave to the caretaker for the care of your pets?

• Can your caretaker afford to take on additional animals?

• What financial expectations does your caretaker have?

If you don't have money, you don't have it, but be prepared if potential caretakers decline to take on a significant financial burden. Even worse, compassionate caretakers may not realize until it is too late how costly this promise is going to be for them to keep.

Kim Hicks of the Arizona Humane Society estimates that it costs approximately $500 annually to properly care for the average cat or dog. In contrast, maintaining horses can cost anywhere from $15,000 to $30,000 a year. The last thing you want is for your animal companions to end up at the pound, a possible result of a caretaker not understanding the financial responsibility of caring for your pets.

At the very least, if money is an issue, work out an informal agreement with a trusted friend or neighbor who shares your passion for animals. Network with local rescue groups and see if you can come to an understanding ahead of time about what will happen to your pets.

Bring in a Third Party

Some people are understandably reluctant about leaving a large sum of money to a family member or friend with seemingly no strings attached. There is a concern that a caretaker could run off with that $15,000 on a wild weekend binge to Atlantic City. A lot is riding on your caretaker's conscience since you cannot require them to spend that money on pet care.

One option you have is to appoint a third party to administer funds to the caretaker for you. Under this plan, the third party agrees to check in on your pets from time to time and give money to the caretaker on a regular basis. This is one method of cutting down on possible caretaker abuse, unless it's the third party who decides to forget about Ginger or Fluffy and blow the $15,000 on a wild weekend binge to Atlantic City.

If your concern is more about sudden long-term illness, rather than your death, consider granting the third party a full power of attorney. This option has become a fairly standard planning device. The person named to act on your behalf under a power of attorney will see that your wishes are carried out while you're incapacitated. You are obligated to provide funds for pet care, maintenance, and veterinary costs. Power of attorney can be prepared to take effect upon your physical or mental incapacity.

Agreeing to serve as a third party watchdog is strictly voluntary and without legal binding. Once again, the pet owner is depending on someone's conscience. Choose wisely.

Decide What Happens When Your Pets Die

If you are going to go to the effort of including your pets in your will and appointing a caretaker, you need to finish the job. What exactly do you expect to happen to your pets' remains when they die? Are they to be cremated, buried, or otherwise taken care of? And how exactly are your wishes going to be financed?

These are all issues for discussion with the caretaker. If you don't make your wishes clear, and if financing hasn't been provided, then everything is left to the whim (and bank account) of the caretaker. Add this to your list and make sure everyone understands your wishes.

Arrange for Short-Term Pet Care

A major drawback to a will where pets are concerned is the potential for a long probate period. There have been cases where it has taken months for a will to be admitted to probate, meaning the health and safety of the animal companions were in limbo. Who is feeding them? Who is taking care of them? There must be specific provisions made to care for your animals during the probate period, most likely through an emergency short-term caretaker, as described in Chapter Three.

Select a Secondary Pet Caretaker

If there is a possibility of you dying, why should your caretaker not be at similar risk? How do you know that your pets may not outlive the caretaker, as well? Nothing about this process is fool-proof, so the only precaution you can take is to appoint a *secondary caretaker* in case something happens to your original designee.

The same criteria apply to selecting both people. There is also the need to educate the secondary caretaker about your animals and your expectations after you die. Additionally, should something happen to your primary caretaker, there must be some notification process in place to alert the secondary caretaker of what has happened.

Do not wait too long before you select your caretakers— approach them as soon as possible. Get something in writing. Do not wait until the last minute, or be forced to make decisions at a time of great personal tragedy. Cover the whole scenario in detail now so there won't be any unresolved questions.

Choosing a Pet Caretaker

Remember, in choosing a pet caretaker:

- Find a good candidate.
- Introduce your pets to the caretaker.
- Prepare your pet caretaker.
- Mention your pet caretaker in your will.
- Provide enough money.
- Bring in a third party.
- Decide what will happen when your pets die.
- Arrange for short-term pet care.
- Select a secondary pet caretaker.

Six

What the Law Allows for Protecting Pets

Ross and Judi Becker were the highly respected publishers of *Good Dog!* magazine, two people whose dedication and zeal to animal welfare defy description. Based in Austin, the Texas couple achieved national recognition for their first-rate and detailed coverage of important canine topics and their tireless championing of animal causes in general. The magazine's administrative assistant, Amanda Braziel, said, "Ross and Judi both loved animals. They dedicated their whole lives to them."

The Beckers were killed in an automobile accident just north of Charleston, South Carolina on June 14, 2001. They were en route to a fiftieth anniversary celebration for Ross's parents. The couple had no children, but they did leave two dogs and five cats back in Austin.

Despite building their professional and personal lives around compassion for animals, the Beckers had made no emergency provisions for their own seven animals. That meant a family member or close friend would have to step in and sort things out. Fortunately, Amanda Braziel was able to handle both her profound grief and her overwhelming concern for the care of the Becker animals. Having worked with the couple for five years and having served as one of their regular pet sitters gave Braziel an important advantage. She knew the pets. They knew her. Their bond was firmly established. The task fell upon Amanda to find new homes for all seven pets and she found herself depending heavily on Becker family members and friends.

The two dogs, Chops and Katie, were elderly, and Amanda convinced her mother and stepfather that they really did need two additional dogs on the family farm. The five cats were not as easy to place. Ross Becker had an old friend who lived in South Carolina. A few years ago, the friend needed to place a cat and Becker volunteered without hesitation. Now the friend decided to return the favor and he adopted Jetski, a jet-black feline.

Meanwhile, Ariel was sent to live with Josh, Judi's adult son from a previous marriage. The Beckers had only recently taken in Molly from friends who were concerned about the cat around a baby. After the accident, the friends agreed to take Molly back. Amanda herself ended up keeping Murphy the Maine coon. That left Boo Radley, another Maine coon who went to Detroit to live with Ross's brother, Bill. "He's a great cat," Bill Becker told us. "Boo's a reminder of how much love and generosity of spirit Ross and Judi showed to animals."

Amanda was there for the Becker pets in their time of need. But for the rest of us, what would happen to our pets if we were to die as suddenly, and as tragically, as Ross and Judi?

In the past, the primary legal option for caring for a pet after your death involved a traditional will (see "Sample Will Pet Provision" in Resources). You consulted with an attorney and left specific instructions about what would happen to your pet after you died. Typically, you had about five options:

• Request your veterinarian to place your pet up for adoption.

• Request that your pet be delivered to a humane shelter for placement.

• Request that your pet be placed in a pet retirement program or animal sanctuary.

• Request your pet be given as a gift to a specific individual.

• Request your veterinarian to euthanize your pet.

Now imagine this scenario: you die tomorrow. There's no need to worry about your two cats, one dog, and one parrot. You made sure that they were provided for in your will. Yet there's that slippery slope called probate to navigate. It can take days, weeks, even months for a court to formally recognize and execute your final requests. And if a relative decides to challenge your will, well, things can get complicated—and prolonged—rather quickly.

Meanwhile, what is happening to your animal companions while all this legal maneuvering unfolds? You thought it would be enough to cover them in your will. Many times it is, but there's that "Twilight Zone" phase for all too many pets whose lives and futures are placed on hold while the estate limps through probate.

～

A statewide survey of wills left behind by Iowa residents discovered provisions made for Mr. Pig, a 150-pound hog; Calamity Jane, a German shepherd; and Chico, an Amazon parrot.

～

Pet Trusts

During the last decade or so, another legal option has emerged in a growing number of states. A *pet trust* is a trust created by the owner for the continual care and safety of a particular animal, or animals. There must be a *trustee* appointed to administer the trust, and some type of money or property must be bequeathed in order to fund the pet trust.

Prior to 1990, many courts refused to recognize the validity of binding pet trusts, primarily because there was no human beneficiary involved to actually enforce the trust. Your parrot may perhaps be able to pontificate profusely, but if something happened to you, your feathered friend is obviously incapable of making sure the terms of your trust are carried out. Pets are property, the courts reasoned.

Instead, the most discretion courts historically granted consisted of *honorary pet trusts*, which were merely advisory. Let's say Mrs. Smith died and it was her sincere wish that her favorite parrot Benjamin be cared for with the $5,000 bequeathed in her will. However, there was no legal obligation for Mrs. Smith's request to be granted. If her trustee didn't share her passion for parrots, then the funds set aside for Benjamin could be transferred back to the estate and dispersed elsewhere. The trustee had complete discretion and someone could die without knowing for certain what would happen to the pets at home.

Some of this judicial reluctance also stems from the *Rule Against Perpetuities*, that says, "No interest in a property is good unless it must vest, if at all, not later than twenty-one years, plus period of gestation, after some life or lives in being at time of creation of interest."

Translation: In order for a trust to be valid, the law requires that disposition of trust property must be settled no later than twenty-one years after the death of the *measuring life*, a person who was alive when the trust was initially created. According to the courts, an animal's life could not be used as the measuring life.

Changes in the Law

Recognizing the ever-increasing human-animal bond, the

National Conference of Commissioners on Uniform State Laws gave a giant boost to the pet trust movement in 1990 when they revised the Uniform Probate Code (UPC) to address, in part, the "concern of many pet owners by providing them a means for leaving funds to be used for the pet's care."

Under the terms of section 2-907, the UPC recognizes assets transferred in trust for the benefit of a pet as a valid, enforceable trust arrangement. A trustee must administer the trust, and make specific distributions for the benefit of the pet. The trust terminates when no living animal is covered by the trust.

If the trustee was unable or unwilling to serve, the court was to appoint a successor trustee. The code was again revised in 1993 to make clear that no assets of the pet trust were to revert for the benefit of the trustee. These combined changes to the UPC made it clear that a pet trust was legally valid in and of itself and no longer merely honorary in nature. The revisions maintained the authority to limit the assets of a particular pet trust to what a judge considered "a reasonable amount."

However, and this is a critical point, section 2-907 only applies in states that either adopt the UPC provision or similar legislation validating pet trusts. So if you live in Illinois, an example of a state that has yet to get on the bandwagon, a trust for your pet is not valid. The interest expressed by state legislatures in validating pet trusts has varied. Some have wholeheartedly embraced the concept. Others continue to recognize only honorary pet trusts. The majority of states still have no law allowing you to legally create a trust to care for your pets.

Summary of State Statutes

Sixteen states have adopted statutes that enable you to create trusts for pets. Four of these states—Nevada, New Jersey, Oregon, and Washington—did so in the first half of 2001. The following is the legal scorecard:

• Six states have adopted language reflecting that of Uniform Probate Code § 2-907 that validates trusts for pets and allows them to continue for the life of the animal: **Alaska, Arizona, Michigan, Montana, New Mexico, and Utah.**

• Five states have adopted statutes that, while not using the exact language of Uniform Probate Code § 2-907, nevertheless validate pet trusts and allow them to continue for the life of the animal: **California, Nevada, North Carolina, Oregon, and Washington.**

• Two states, **Missouri** and **Tennessee**, recognize pet trusts but treat them the same as honorary trusts, valid only for twenty-one years or less.

• Two states, **New Jersey** and **New York**, allow pet trusts that terminate when no living animal is covered by the trust, or at the end of twenty-one years, whichever occurs first.

• One state, **Colorado**, not only allows trusts for pets to continue for the life of the animal, but for the lives of any animals in gestation at the time the trust begins.

• One state, **Pennsylvania**, has yet to adopt a specific statute enforcing pet trusts or honorary trusts, but the Keystone State has an animal-friendly court system whose judges have historically ruled in favor of bequests left for specific animals, a precedent spun from common law.

• One state, **Wisconsin**, has an honorary trust statute that does not specifically refer to pets but permits an individual to apply trust property to any purpose that is not capricious.

• One state, **Oregon**, exempts pets from the probate process, expediting their legal transfer to humane societies or new owners.

s the language of Uniform Probate Code § 2-907: "A
are of a designated domestic or pet animal is valid. The
tes when no living animal is covered by the trust."

N

 to Title 11 Revised Code of Washington Effective

izes trusts that are established for the benefit of
ng, "A trust for the care of one or more animals is
imals that are to be benefited by the trust may be
dentified, or may be identified in such other manner
be readily identified. Unless otherwise provided in
rument or in this chapter, the trust will terminate
nal that is designated as a beneficiary of the trust
g."

dan of Seattle Animal Control serves on the gov-
for the Washington State Federation of Animal Care
Agencies. Jordan says his colleagues were pleased
Washington pet trust legislation was signed into
finally acknowledged the fact that if a person wants
llion to a cat, he or she can do it. Prior to this, people
rovisions, but there wasn't any legal guarantee. Now

lation

ement toward the validation of pet trusts continues.
J.S. Congressman Earl Blumenauer (D-OR) officially
islation that would raise the issue of pet trusts for
ration. Blumenauer's bill, the "Charitable Pet Trusts
alls for a new section to be added to the Internal
allowing for the creation of charitable trusts for pets
nder interest passes to a qualified charity. In addi-
ction also mirrors the current language for existing

State Pet Trust Statutes

ALASKA

Alaska Stat. § 13.12.907 Honorary trusts; trusts for pets

Mirrors the language of Uniform Probate Code § 2-907: "A
trust for the care of a designated domestic or pet animal is valid. The
trust terminates when no living animal is covered by the trust."

ARIZONA

A.R.S. § 14-2907 Honorary trusts; trust for pets; conditions

Mirrors the language of Uniform Probate Code § 2-907: "A
trust for the care of a designated domestic or pet animal is valid. The
trust terminates when no living animal is covered by the trust."

CALIFORNIA

Cal Prob Code § 15212 Duration of trust for care of animal

States: "...A trust for the care of a designated domestic or pet
animal may be performed by the trustee for the life of the animal..."

COLORADO

C.R.S. § 15-11-901 Honorary trusts; trusts for pets

States: "...a trust for the care of designated domestic or pet
animals and the animals' offspring in gestation is valid." The
determination of "animals' offspring in gestation" is made at the
time the animals become beneficiaries of the trust, and the trust
ends "when no living animal is covered by the trust."

MICHIGAN

MCLS § 700.2722 Honorary trusts; trusts for pets

Mirrors the language of Uniform Probate Code § 2-907: "A
trust for the care of a designated domestic or pet animal is valid. The
trust terminates when no living animal is covered by the trust."

MISSOURI
R.S.Mo. § 456-055 Honorary trusts—pet animals—noncharitable societies

Treats pet trusts the same as honorary trusts, valid only for twenty-one years or less.

MONTANA
Mont. Code Anno., § 72-2-1017 Honorary trusts—trusts for pets

Mirrors the language of Uniform Probate Code § 2-907: "A trust for the care of a designated domestic or pet animal is valid. The trust terminates when no living animal is covered by the trust."

NEVADA
Addition to Chapter 163 of Nevada Revised Statutes Effective October 1, 2001

Expressly validates a trust for the care of an animal, stating, "A trust created for the care of one or more animals that are alive at the time of the settlor's death is valid. Such a trust terminates upon the death of all animals covered by the terms of the trust."

NEW JERSEY
Supplement to Title 3B of New Jersey Permanent Statutes § 3B:11-38 Effective July 10, 2001

Recognizes the validity of trust funds for pets, stating, "A trust for the care of a domesticated animal is valid...The trust shall terminate when no living animal is covered by the trust, or at the end of 21 years, whichever occurs earlier."

NEW MEXICO
N.M. Stat. Ann. § 45-2-907 Honorary trusts; trusts for pets

Mirrors the language of Uniform Probate Code § 2-907: "A trust for the care of a designated domestic or pet animal is valid. The trust terminates when no living animal is covered by the trust."

NEW YORK
NY CLS EPTL § 7-6.1 Honora

States: "A trust for the ca animal is valid...Such trust sh mal is covered by the trust, o whichever occurs earlier."

NORTH CAROLINA
N.C. Gen. Stat. § 36A-147 Tru

States: "...a trust for th domestic or pet animals alive is valid... The trust terminate surviving animal. "

OREGON
New Provision to Oregon Re 27, 2001

States: "Any person ma designated domestic or pet a the care of individually nam but any animal provided for time of the trustor's death...I vision for termination of th living animal is covered by exhausted, whichever occur

TENNESSEE
Tenn. Code Ann. § 35-50-1

Treats pet trusts the s twenty-one years or less.

UTAH
Utah. Code Ann. § 75-2-1(

Mirro trust for the trust termin

WASHINGT(
New Chapt July 22, 200

Recog animals, stat valid. The a individually that they car the trust ins when no ani remains livir

Don Jo erning board and Control when the ne law. "The stat to leave $1 m were making there is."

Federal Legis
The mo In May 2001, introduced le federal consid Act of 2001," Revenue Code when the rem tion, the new s

charitable trusts and includes provisions designed to prevent fraud.

The legislation, HR 1796, if passed, allows pet owners to set up planned giving arrangements to benefit their animals; a trust could be set up to care for a specific pet as long as he or she lives. Federal taxpayers are given the opportunity to establish and accrue the tax benefits of pet trusts, whether or not their state of residence already recognizes such trusts.

In introducing the legislation, Representative Blumenauer said, "Whether it's a dog, cat, or rabbit, pets, or 'companion animals' bring great joy and contentment to their owners throughout their lives. Pet owners from coast to coast are anxious to ensure the safety, well-being and health of these important companions. This legislation allows them to do so and offers an important measure of comfort to those seeking to ensure the proper care for their long time friend."

In a September 2001 interview with *The New York Times*, Blumenauer elaborated on his reasons for introducing the bill. He recalled his time as a county commissioner in Portland where animal control was a constant concern.

He believes that society is of two minds about pets. "We profess great love for companion animals; we have nearly sixty million cats and almost as many dogs. We all know people for whom animals are a huge part of their lives. But we are less than stellar in what we do with unattended animals."

Blumenauer's bill has already come under some criticism. J. J. MacNab, a Maryland-based insurance industry analyst, took the Oregon representative to task after the pet trust legislation was introduced. "On the surface, Representative Blumenauer's bill seems as harmless as a toy poodle," said MacNab. "But the bill is as dangerous as it is silly. It is an open invitation for those who abuse charities to make a fortune on its weaknesses. What's more, it makes a mockery of more important issues on which Congress needs to be spending its time and attention."

MacNab worries that the legislation provides a monetary incentive to keep a suffering pet alive well beyond the point where others might be inclined to show compassion. Also, there is the issue of fraud to consider. "Because payments from a charitable trust are based on life expectancy, pet trusts could be abused by manipulating the 'lifetime' of the animal that the trust purportedly benefits," MacNab argues.

Blumenauer sounds a more optimistic tone. "This bill will allow everyone to set up a pet trust and not be a burden on society. My intention was to get it on the radar screen now and use it as a vehicle for people around the country who really care about this issue."

In May 2001, HR 1796 was referred to the House Ways and Means Committee for further consideration, where it remains as of early 2002. Stay tuned.

SEVEN

The Courts: Friend or Foe?

Howard Brand of South Burlington, Vermont died January 2, 1999 at the age of 88. His attorney, John C. Fitzpatrick of Montpelier, was appointed executor of the estate. Included in the Brand will was a specific provision detailing the fate of his four horses: "If at the time of my death I am still the owner of my animals, including my horses, I direct my Executor to have such animals destroyed."

By all accounts, Brand, a longtime farmer and trucker, treated his horses with compassion. According to Fitzpatrick, his client worried that the horses might fall victim to inhumane treatment in the hands of others—better to have them destroyed, he felt. Brand supposedly also ordered the destruction of his Cadillac, the demolition of which was to be carried out in the presence of Fitzpatrick.

Word leaked out, however, and Mary Ingham stepped into the picture. Her uncle was the caretaker on the Brand property and Ingham had previously owned one of the horses. A tanning salon employee, she visited the animals regularly and was quite upset to learn of Brand's final wishes. Ingham scraped together $2,500 for legal fees and mounted a two-month crusade to save the horses with the assistance of a band of Vermont humane societies who formed the Coalition to Save Brand's Horses.

Ingham and her supporters filed a legal challenge against the destruction of the horses, asking the probate judge instead to spare their lives. The judge faced an important question: *Can someone request that a healthy animal be destroyed as part of his or her final will?*

After hearing arguments on both sides, Judge Susan Fowler issued a decision March 17, 1999. Though recognizing the sanctity of a person's will, Judge Fowler ruled that Vermont's policy against inhumane treatment of animals outweighed Brand's final request.

In part, the judge reasoned, "Our social history and cultural development illustrate an increasing understanding of the rights of nonhuman animals.... It would seem to this court that a death sentence imposed upon healthy, if aging, animals might be considered cruel in its own right. Consequently...Vermont law should operate to allow these animals the opportunity to continue living."

Still, in deference to Brand's obvious concern about his horses should they live, Judge Fowler instructed the court to oversee the placement of the animals and approve any final transfer of ownership. Dozens of phone calls soon came in from people volunteering to take the animals. Ingham's caretaker uncle disagreed with the court challenge and no longer speaks to his neice, however, Ingham considers her $2,500 well spent. The horses lived. The Cadillac, however, was not as fortunate.

For more than 250 years, British and American courts have wrestled with fundamental issues relating to pet ownership and what the law allows in terms of wills and pet trusts. Unfortunately, as legal scholar Barbara Schwartz noted in 1974, "Historically, the approach of most American courts towards bequests for the care of specific animals has not been calculated to gladden the hearts of animal lovers."

What is the problem? Basically, it is the fact that American courts have not allowed pets to inherit money or property directly. This is a point worth repeating: *the courts have not allowed pets to inherit money or property directly.* The judicial reasoning is pretty straightforward. That slobbering basset hound perched on your lap may be your best friend, but the court views the dog strictly as property. Animals, by law, are property, and one piece of property cannot own another piece of property; therefore, pets cannot be named as direct beneficiaries of either a will or a trust.

Harvard law professor Steven Wise, author of *Rattling the Cage: Towards Legal Rights for Animals,* says this attitude towards animals dates back more than four thousand years, creating what Wise calls "a thick and impenetrable legal wall" that separates all human from nonhuman animals.

> On one side, even the most trivial interests of a single species—ours—are jealously guarded. On the other side of that wall lies the legal refuse of an entire kingdom...gorillas, monkeys, dogs, and dolphins. They are "legal things." Their most basic and fundamental interests—their pains, their lives, their freedoms—are intentionally ignored, often maliciously trampled and routinely abused.

> Ancient philosophers claimed that all nonhuman animals had been designed and placed on this earth just for human beings. Ancient jurists declared that law had been created just for human beings. Although philosophy and science have long since recanted, the law has not.

Trying to break through that wall may be difficult. Choosing to protect your pet through some type of formal legal mechanism, such as a will or a trust, throws you at the mercy of judges, attorneys, and trust officers who may not love pets as much as you do. Remember, even if you meticulously prepare all the required documents, dotting every "i" and crossing every "t," there is still no guarantee that your wishes will be followed.

Regardless, some people have tried to leave money or property to their pets, often prompting some type of challenge from incredulous and jealous relatives at the probate hearing. In one case an elderly woman's will was challenged by a local community foundation. Leo Grillo of D.E.L.T.A. (Dedication & Everlasting Love To Animals) Rescue in Southern California appeared in probate court a few years ago after a woman left a rather large bequest to this animal rescue organization. Imagine Grillo's surprise to hear the community foundation lawyers challenge the bequest by arguing that leaving money to animals was proof that the woman had to be crazy. Then imagine Grillo's surprise to hear the judge side with the community foundation; D.E.L.T.A. was out-maneuvered.

Thus, if you leave something to a pet in your will, there is a risk it will go to an alternate beneficiary instead, or lacking that, to your nearest relatives. Your pet will not always be protected.

That is exactly what happened in California when Thelma Russell died. Her will was inscribed on a small card: "I leave everything I own Real & Personal to Chester H. Quinn & Roxy Russell." Chester was a good friend, but Roxy Russell turned out to be an Airedale. Russell's niece, Georgia Nan Russell, challenged the will (*In re Estate of Russell*, 1968) and the California Supreme Court voided the gift to the dog, decreeing, "A dog cannot be the beneficiary under a will." Since Georgia was the only living heir, she received Roxy's half of the estate, even though Thelma Russell specifically told Quinn that she did not want her niece to get anything. Good intentions are not enough in the eyes of the law; a pet simply cannot be named the beneficiary in a will. It has been this way for quite a long time.

At the Mercy of the Courts

Judicial thinking on what people can legally leave their pets dates back to English common law. British courts have long approved gifts directed to support specific animals. Unfortunately, American courts have embraced a more conservative approach, often hampering those who just wish to do the right thing. Typical of this line of reasoning was the argument by the Texas Court of Appeals in *Arrington v. Arrington* (1981) when the justices wrote, "A dog, for all its admirable and unique qualities, is not a human being and is not treated in the law as such."

The first known court case in the United States dealing with a gift for the benefit of a specific pet, *Willett v. Willett* (1923), came from Kentucky, and involved a dog named Dick whose owner bequeathed the dog $1,000 in a will. The intent of the owner was to help insure that Dick would receive three meals daily, have a bed in the house by the fire, and be treated well every day.

Family members challenged the bequest, however, and the lower court rejected any gift to Dick because the owner failed to name a specific trustee and because a dog, under Kentucky law, was not allowed to be the recipient of a gift. The Kentucky Court of Appeals later reversed the lower court ruling and held that the pet owner's desire to care for her dog was a "humane purpose" and thus valid.

The judges wrote, in part:

> It is insisted, and the lower court so held, that the bequest for the support of the dog Dick must fail because (1) there is no trustee, and (2) a dog cannot take as devisee under our law. It must be remembered that equity never allows a trust to fail for want of a

trustee. The court can and should appoint a trustee to take and carry out the trust in favor of the dog.

The Willett decision seemed a promising start, but as law professor Gerry Beyer argues in his historical analysis, "This auspicious beginning was not generally followed. Not until the late twentieth century did the tide towards effectuating a pet owner's desire to care for pets after the owner's death begin to rise again."

Various reasons, mostly technical, account for judicial apathy towards pet bequests. We already know the law considers pets to be property and unable to inherit directly. Courts also are never reluctant to step in and slash bequests to animals that they consider excessive. Others have interpreted the language of such requests to be completely honorary or non-binding, meaning it is up to the beneficiary to decide if the pets are cared for, or not. And sometimes the courts have had little choice because the pet owner made a mistake and didn't follow proper procedure. In the Arkansas case of *Dailey v. Adams* (1959), the court voided an agreement to care for a deceased person's animals, in part due to a missing signature.

Yet it is important to stress that the courts have not spoken with one voice. In truth, when confronted with a dead owner and a surviving pet, judges respond in various ways. Some have followed the strict letter of the law and not allowed any discretion. Others have discovered the animal within them, seeking more creative ways of implementing the apparent wishes of the deceased, even sometimes looking the other way legally.

Hundreds of court cases followed in the wake of *Willett v. Willett*. A few of the more prominent decisions are worth mentioning to illustrate key legal issues the courts have considered in assessing the plight of companion animals after their owners have died.

A Gift But Not a Trust

John Renner, who died in 1946, left his dog and his parrot to Mary Faiss Reising. His will seemed quite specific:

> All the rest, residue and remainder of my estate, real and personal, of whatsoever kind and wheresoever situate, I give, devise and bequeath unto my executrix, hereinafter named, IN TRUST, however, for the maintenance of my pets, which I leave to her kind care and judgment, and for their interment upon their respective deaths in Francisvale Cemetery.

However, Renner's niece and nephew challenged the trust in court, arguing that they were the rightful heirs and that Renner's trust was invalid. The case came before the Supreme Court of Pennsylvania (*In re Renner's Estate*, 1948). The court eventually rejected the claims of the niece and nephew and upheld the spirit of Renner's request, saying in part:

> His will meant that the executrix should take the residue from that time; he wished her to apply as much as she considered necessary to the care of the pets and to retain the rest for her own use.

However, the state court also ruled that Renner's instructions to his friend constituted a gift, not a trust, and therefore no precedent was set for the legality of pet trusts. Reising was left to do with the estate, including the two pets, as she wished. Whether or not the dog and the parrot were properly cared for, the court concluded, was dependent solely on Reising's compassion and loyalty, not judicial oversight.

An Honorary Pet Trust

Mr. Searight left the following instructions in his will:

> I give and bequeath my dog, Trixie, to Florence Hand
> of Wooster, Ohio, and I direct my executor to deposit in
> the Peoples Federal Savings and Loan Association,
> Wooster, Ohio, the sum of $1000.00 to be used by him
> to pay Florence Hand at the rate of 75 cents per day for
> the keep and care of my dog as long as it shall live.

No relatives stepped forward to challenge Searight's will in probate, but the Department of Taxation of Ohio did try to block the bequest (*In re Searight's Estate*, 1950). The probate court had decided that the $1,000 would not be subject to state inheritance tax. Officials wanted the state court to invalidate Trixie's gift in order to collect additional taxes.

The Ohio court refused, showing a kinder and gentler approach to animals by becoming one of the first to recognize an "honorary pet trust" as being legal and valid:

> Text writers on the subject of trusts designate a bequest
> for the care of a specific animal as an "honorary trust"
> —that is, one binding on the conscience of the trustee,
> since there is no beneficiary capable of enforcing the
> trust...Modern authorities uphold the validity of a gift
> for the purpose designated...where the person to whom
> the power is given is willing to carry out the testator's
> wishes. Whether called an honorary trust, or whatever
> terminology is used, we conclude that the bequest for
> the dog, Trixie, is not in and of itself unlawful.

The use of honorary pet trusts has become a popular judicial mechanism for permitting estate arrangements that benefit animals. An honorary pet trust is exempted from traditional regulations, such as the Rule Against Perpetuities, so it allows judges an escape if their intent is to look the other way, ignore the law, and focus on protecting a particular animal's welfare.

∼

In the New Jersey case of Greenwood v. Henry *(1894), an attorney pointed out that the will in question could not be a forgery because it contained provisions for Jenny the horse and two dogs, Fox and Rover. A forger would not have included "such foolish provisions," the attorney argued.*

∼

A "Patently Unsupportable" Bequest

A Pennsylvania woman named Florence B. Lyons set aside a substantial portion of her $1.4 million estate, approximately $50,000 a year, to care for her four horses and six dogs. Upon the death of these animals, the balance of the estate was to go to Princeton University for a scholarship fund.

Upon reviewing the will, the court found the large bequest to be honorary, but "patently unsupportable," and theorized that Lyons had somehow miscalculated how much money was actually needed to care for all her animals (*In re Lyons' Estate*, 1974):

> There is language in this will that suggests that Mrs. Lyons might not have had any idea how much it would cost to maintain the animals nor perhaps even how large her estate might be. It is reasonable to suppose, however, that she did not intend her entire estate to be tied up for the lives of the animals if less than the full estate was necessary for the purpose.

The court instead authorized a maximum of $150,000 to be used for the animals and placed them under the care of a local humane society. The balance of the estate was granted immediately to Princeton University.

A decade later, the Pennsylvania court again slashed a trust bequest for two cats that it considered to be excessive (*In re Templeton Estate*, 1984). The justices wrote, "The court uses its inherent power to reduce the amount involved…to an amount which is sufficient to accomplish the owner's purpose."

The message is loud and clear. You can leave money for your pets, but it must be reasonable. If a judge considers it excessive, there may be little hesitation in reducing the amount.

An Enforceable Trust

Doris Duke, the only child of tobacco baron James Buchanan Duke who founded Duke University and the American Tobacco Company, died of a morphine overdose in her Beverly Hills mansion in 1993. She was 80 years old and left behind an estate valued at more than $1 billion. Her will detailed everything to be done with her property in exactly twenty-one paragraphs.

Toward the end of the will, the reclusive Duke announced her intent to establish a $100,000 trust fund for her mutt, Minni, with the stipulation that the dog should be cared for by an appointed caretaker, Mariano DeVelasco, and they would live at Falcon's Lair, Duke's stately Beverly Hills mansion. It is interesting to note that two other dogs belonging to Duke—Kimo, a German shepherd mix, and Chairman Mao, a sharpei—were not mentioned in the will, though they continued to live at the heiress' Rhode Island estate.

Minni's trust fund was challenged in New York probate court by the estate's executor, the Doris Duke Charitable Foundation, which objected to such a lavish sum of money being left to a dog

(*In re Estate of Duke*, 1997). Foundation attorneys argued this was an unenforceable trust because there was no human beneficiary. Since Duke died three years prior to the signing of the New York pet trust legislation in 1996, the new law did not apply to this case.

Nevertheless, Judge Eve Preminger ruled in favor of DeVelasco and Minni, agreeing that the trust provisions Duke established were indeed enforceable.

> By separating the legal ownership of the trust fund…
> and the legal ownership of the dog…a valid trust is
> created of which Mr. DeVelasco is beneficiary. By
> relieving the dog owner of financial burden which he
> would otherwise incur, the trust benefits the dog
> owner and he is therefore properly characterized as a
> beneficiary who may enforce the trust.

You do not have to have the millions of Doris Duke to win in court, but the lesson here is clear. Be careful and specific in the wording of your pet trust so that it will hold up against any potential legal challenges that might emerge after you are gone.

A Gift of Life

Like Howard Brand, the Vermont farmer who wanted his horses to die with him, there are still many misguided pet owners who insist that their animals not outlive them. Unfortunately, their idea of pet estate planning is a bullet between the eyes. These people are neither uncaring nor barbaric. Most of them love their animals dearly, but somehow they are convinced that their pets will suffer in the hands of others. They reason that it is better to spare their animal companions a fate of suffering, "so, when I go, they go."

Fortunately, the courts have not always agreed. One of the

most famous cases involved Ida M. Capers, a Pennsylvania woman whose will directed her executors to destroy "in a humane manner" her two Irish setters, Sunny Birch and Brickland. According to court documents, Capers feared that the dogs would grieve for her and that no other person could possibly offer the affection she had shown them.

Shortly before entering the hospital for the final time, Capers left both dogs in the care of Thomas and Dolores Miller, who owned a nursery and also operated a small kennel. After Capers died, the executors sought to carry out her wishes, but the Millers refused to surrender the dogs.

The Millers' fight to protect Sunny Birch and Brickland soon captured the hearts of animal lovers around the country. An article appeared in *Life* magazine. The mayor of Pittsburgh defended the dogs and even Governor William Scranton, who then was eyeing a presidential run in 1964, directed his attorney general to intervene on the dogs' behalf.

A hearing was held in September 1964 in the courtroom of Judge William S. Rahauser (*In re Capers Estate*, 1964). The Millers clearly had no legal standing in this case and there appeared to be nothing on the surface to invalidate Capers' will. But the letters came pouring in from across the country, begging Rahauser to spare the dogs' lives.

In his opinion, the judge wrote that euthanizing the two dogs would serve no purpose; instead it would be seen as an act of "cruelty" and "gross inhumanity." Pets may be property, he reasoned, but no one has the right in this case to destroy property. Rahauser also commented on the considerable public opinion surrounding the case, saying:

> ...There is a positive, well-defined and universal public sentiment, deeply integrated in the customs and beliefs of the people of this era, opposed to the unnecessary

destruction of animals…There is no lack of care [for the dogs]. There is no reason for carrying out the literal provision of the will. That decedent would rather see her pets happy and healthy and alive than destroyed, there can be no doubt.

Judge Rahauser ordered Sunny Birch and Brickland to be placed in the care of the Western Pennsylvania Humane Society; to no one's surprise, the Millers adopted both dogs shortly thereafter.

The Capers decision is not an isolated case. Recently, a report by the State Bar of Nevada recently concluded, "Providing for pet euthanasia upon the owner's death is almost never a good idea and may not even be considered humane."

A California court reached a similar conclusion in *Smith v. Avanzino* (1980) when the San Francisco SPCA intervened and refused to follow an estate's directive to euthanize a dog. The general public and humane societies are becoming increasingly aggressive on this issue, while the courts appear more and more sympathetic to the plight of the animals. Such a powerful combination spells trouble for anyone unwilling to give their animals a second chance at love with someone else.

EIGHT

Setting Up a Pet Trust

It has been an emotional roller coaster for Douglas Brown, a gruff, British-born woodworker now living in California. Patty, his beloved wife of thirty-two years, died suddenly, unexpectedly, the previous month, following two long months of hospitalization. She was only 56. One minute she was smiling, then she was off to the hospital, complaining of headaches and an upset stomach.

But Douglas isn't the only one in this house confused and grieving over the loss of Patty. There are also the three cats— Dorianne, Norman, and Mama Cass.

"They knew from day one that Patty wasn't right," Douglas mutters. "Then she went missing and they went really, really strange. They began to tear up her chair. They still don't go on it. They just look up at it, expecting to see Patty, and, of course, she's not there. And they're totally confused."

Douglas sighs as he plops on his couch. "Patty's always been a cat person. I don't really like them." This from a man trapped in a house surrounded by cat kitsch. Magnets on the refrigerator, a cat toaster cover, and two cat "Welcome" signs at the front door.

Eight separate cat drawings hang in the kitchen and living room. Cat salt and pepper shakers on the table and a cat planter in the front window, near the cat calendar on the wall.

While Douglas talks, his three cats wander through the living room and nearby porch. Mama Cass is a gray tabby. Dorianne, a manx, has yellow eyes and a dark gray coat. Norman looks to be a large, black, medium-haired furball. They were Patty's cats, Douglas insists. She had cats around constantly, even when they were living in England. Douglas knew better than to argue with her.

But now it is just Douglas and the three amigos. He tries to be sympathetic to their plight. "They've really stayed inside a lot, more than they ever did before, especially Norman," Douglas explains with a sigh. "He doesn't go out now, whereas before, he was out all the time. They're just annoyed that she's not here."

Patty Brown loved her three cats dearly, but she failed to make any just-in-case emergency provisions for them. Now the task has fallen to Douglas. He mumbles and grumbles about all this new responsibility.

～

The standoff between Douglas and the cats didn't last long. Within the year, Douglas met and moved in with another woman, in another house, in another town, without any cats. A friend adopted Mama Cass. However, Dorianne and Norman ran away.

Patty Brown would be heartbroken to learn the fate of her cats, but this is what can happen if you do not prepare or when you assume that someone else will take care of everything. You cannot always depend on others, not even a spouse. If you love your animals, then you owe it to them to set up some legal and financial security should something terrible happen.

The most reliable method, in consultation with your attorney, is a pet trust that sets up a trustee and a caretaker, and provides for a reasonable distribution of funds to care for your animals after you are gone. Often, pet trusts are set up as part of a revocable family trust. As your attorney will remind you, there are certain tax laws that must be followed. And you must live in a state that recognizes pet trusts (see Chapter Six). Otherwise you must choose another method to care for your pets, such as leaving your pets and a sum of money in your will to a trusted friend or family member who has agreed to step in.

Though a pet trust is a relatively straightforward piece of business, its strength lies in your careful planning and consideration of a number of key issues.

∼

Even the most dedicated caregiver can turn out to be less than honest. Law professor Gerry Beyer cites one case where a maid who inherited the care of her employer's cat kept the money flowing after the cat's death by simply buying a replacement animal.

∼

Living Trust Versus Testamentary Trust

We have already discussed the use of honorary pet trusts, a mechanism recognized by some courts but without real bite since everything is left to the discretion of the trustee. If your trustee decides to spend the money otherwise, there is no legal protection for your animals; everything is based on your faith in the trustee.

Instead, you can consider either an *inter vivos* trust, also known as a living trust, or you can opt for a testamentary trust. A living trust is something you can establish now, today, and it takes effect immediately, meaning it will already be in place when you die. A living trust can be revocable, allowing you to modify or terminate it at any time.

The primary advantage of a living trust is that it circumvents the delay between your death and the probating of your will, a period that may run weeks or months. Since a living trust does not have to go through probate, your caretaker has immediate access to any funds required for the safety and well-being of your animals.

However, this option is not without drawbacks. Since you are setting up a living trust today, that means you must transfer to it today funds or property you wish to leave for the care of your animals. You may, however, choose to establish a living trust with a nominal amount of money, arranging for more to be transferred in from a bank account or insurance policy after your will goes through probate. You have to decide how quickly your pets will need financial support.

A living trust may have additional start-up and administrative expenses as well. Some pet owners simply don't want to tie up their assets in a trust while they are still alive; this idea of "pay

---

Comparison of Pet Trust Options

A Living Trust
• Takes effect immediately.
• Allows you to make changes easily as needed.
• Avoids probate and any delay in caring for your pets.

A Testamentary Trust
• Takes effect after you die.
• Avoids any type of property or fund transfer prior to your death.
• Must be probated and is subject to judicial review.

---

in advance" may not appeal to you.

A testamentary trust does not take effect until after you die and your will has gone through probate, so it is more like "pay after you're gone." Some favor this option because it does not require any immediate transfer of assets into the trust. But a testamentary trust is part of your will, which must be probated, making you account-able to the courts and running the risk of delay.

Pet Trusts: The Ten Basic Steps

No two pet trusts are exactly the same. Individual needs vary, as do state regulations. Still, when you sit down with your attorney to prepare your pet trust, your wishes are most likely to be realized if you follow ten basic steps.

Step One: Select a Trustee

A pet trust is administered by a trustee, either an individual or a corporation. Your attorney can serve as your trustee; so could your bank. Either one is probably a safe choice. Perhaps you prefer a family member or trusted friend. Some trusts have the same person as both trustee and caretaker. While that is easier and less time consuming, having one person do both negates any checks and balances on the trust process. It is best to keep these functions separate. Make sure your trustee has an appreciation for animals in general, and especially your animals.

If you have enough money in the trust, offer to pay the trustee. Go the extra step and appoint a secondary trustee should something unfortunate happen to your first choice. According to the *Times-Union*, in Albany, New York, it should cost less than $1,000 in legal fees to establish a pet trust.

Step Two: Select a Pet Caretaker

Fill in the blank: If something happened to me, I would want __(NAME)__ to take care of my animals. You now have your first choice for a pet caretaker. In Chapter Five, we outline the qualities of a good caretaker. Those principles apply here when you designate the person to care for your pets. Make this decision thoughtfully and carefully—your choice of a caretaker will determine the long-term success or failure of your arrangements.

Your caretaker will assume all responsibility of caring for your pets, so it is important to make sure in advance that he or she understands fully the obligation undertaken. Discuss in detail your expectations for the animals and make sure your pets will accept both the caretaker and their new environment.

There is always the chance that something unfortunate might happen to your caretaker; guard against that by selecting one or two secondary caretakers who can step in should the need arise.

Should you pay a pet caretaker? Our advice is yes, if you can afford it, even if only as a token gesture of appreciation.

Step Three: Bequeath Your Animals to the Trustee

Once you have selected a trustee and a caretaker, you need to bequeath the animals to the trustee. It's advisable to include specific instructions as to how your trustee is to take custody of all your animals. Will someone deliver them to the trustee? Is the trustee supposed to pick them up somewhere? And once the trustee has secured the animals, and established their general health, how then does the trustee transfer the animals over to the caretaker? Work all this out in advance.

We hope you have established a Pet Identification System (see Chapter Four). Make sure your trustee knows where to find this material; it will be vital in taking care of the animals. If cats or birds are involved, where do you keep their carriers? Put it in writing.

Step Four: Avoid Excessive Funding

"How much is too much?" That's literally the $64,000 question in setting up a pet trust. You have to determine a dollar amount that will be both sufficient and reasonable—enough to protect your animals, but not so excessive as to invite challenge from either relatives or a judge if your will ends up in dispute.

The task is somewhat easier if you know for sure how old your pets are. You need to be able to calculate some type of life expectancy for each animal, while factoring in annual costs for grooming, food, veterinary care, and the final cost of burial or cremation. Also remember that as an animal ages, typically more medical care is required. Consult your veterinarian for authoritative cost projections. You do have the option of putting in general guidelines as to how you want the money spent.

Do not forget to consider the expenses of your caretaker. Who will step in for the pets if your caretaker leaves on vacation, or needs to board the animals in a kennel? Is it your intention to financially compensate the caretaker? These are all legitimate expenses to consider.

In addition, the size of your trust will be influenced by how many pets are covered in the provisions. If you have ten cats, then $100,000 might seem reasonable. If you have only one cat, then some fur might fly. You should not leave your entire estate for the benefit of your animals. Remember this axiom: *The more money you leave your pets, the greater the chance that the bequest will be challenged.* If the amount of property left to the pet trust seems unreasonable, some court may reduce it to a more acceptable level and increase the amount left to other beneficiaries.

Setting up a pet trust proves you love your animals. However, keep that love in perspective. A big heart is more important than a big trust fund. Do not leave too much money in the trust fund.

Step Five: Request a Desired Standard of Living

There was a pet trustee in Arizona who used money from the estate to buy a new washing machine. He reasoned that it was a necessary expense in order to launder the dog's bed clothing.

Whether this is excessive or not largely depends on the dog's expected standard of living.

You have gone to a great deal of effort to safeguard your animals. Finish the task by considering the quality of life you expect your pets to enjoy. Your caretaker needs a basic idea so that he or she can preserve their quality of life. Are your cats indoors only? What type of food do you feed your parrot? How often are the dogs groomed? Are they exercised daily? Do you spoil them in any way, or reward them with any special treats? Your caretaker needs to know.

Putting this in writing also helps protect your caretaker against potential accusations of reckless spending. A caretaker can easily follow your wishes, assuming you've put them in writing.

Step Six: Set Time Limits on the Trust

A trust should not run forever, so build in an expiration date. If you live in a pet trust friendly state like Alaska or Colorado, you can simply link the length of your trust to the death of your last pet. However, most states do not permit that option, forcing you to make a different calculation. In many states the maximum length of time is twenty-one years. You may be able to use the life of your caretaker or trustee as a measure.

Step Seven: Use the Trustee as a Watchdog

Ask your trustee to make periodic visits to your animals to make sure all is going well with the caretaker. The visits should take place in the animals' new environment to permit an assessment of their physical and psychological well-being. Ideally, such visits should be unannounced.

Step Eight: Provide Complete Identification

We have shared stories with you about dishonest caretakers who tried to keep the checks coming in by going through a series of black dogs or brown tabby cats, swearing that it was still the original animal. There are some basic steps you can take to provide proper identification and avoid such fraud.

First, prepare a list of any unique markings on your pets. For example, our basset hound, Charlie, has a small scar across the bridge of his nose. Include any photographs you have. If dogs are involved, a video might be a good idea, especially if they do certain tricks on command.

Second, have your veterinarian place a microchip in each one of your animals. It is painless and relatively inexpensive. If your trustee becomes concerned at some future date about the identity of an animal, the microchip can be scanned for verification.

Step Nine: Select a Remainder Beneficiary

You decide to set up a trust of $15,000 for your three cats. Within five years of your death, all three cats also die, but there's still $3,500 left in the trust. What happens to that money?

You should name a remainder beneficiary in your trust, preferably an organization that will receive any leftover amount after the last pet has died. We suggest naming a local humane organization or animal rescue group—they can always use the money.

The critical point is that you not leave the balance to your caretaker because of the uneasy financial incentive this creates. If your caretaker gets the balance of the estate upon the death of your pets, what motive does he or she have to make sure the pets are cared for properly? We don't mean to sound like an old Alfred Hitchcock movie, but be safe. Remove temptation. Name someone other than your caretaker as the remainder beneficiary.

Step Ten: Provide Instructions for Final Disposition of Pets

Think about what you want to happen with your animals when they die. Do you want them buried? If so, where? Do you want them cremated? If so, what about their ashes? Do you expect any type of memorial service or tribute to them? And who is going to pay for all this? Spell out your wishes now so that your animals are not neglected later.

One Last Strategy

Consult with your attorney about the appropriateness of an *in terrorem* or "no contest" clause in your will. From the Latin term for "in fear," the *in terrorem* clause is a legal provision that assures if anyone challenges the legality of your will or any part of it, and the challenge fails, then that person gets nothing or only a token amount such as $1, in place of a larger amount they might have received. This strategy can be used to discourage people from challenging any bequests you might leave for your animals. However, in order for such a clause to be potentially effective, you should leave some amount of money to the suspected "challenger." If a family member has no bequest to lose, an *in terrorem* clause may not deter them, but someone might think twice about a possible challenge if $5,000 is at stake. If a will is contested and found to be invalid, then this clause also fails.

Remember, in setting up a pet trust:

- Select a trustee.

- Select a pet caretaker.

- Bequeath your animals to the trustee.

- Avoid excessive funding.

- Request a desired standard of living.

- Set time limits on the trust.

- Use the trustee as a watchdog.

- Provide complete identification.

- Select a remainder beneficiary.

- Provide instructions for final disposition of pets.

NINE

Animal Shelters and Humane Societies

Norman and Diane Pomerance have seven dogs, including a husky, a dachshund, a beagle mix, and a German shepherd. The husband and wife, both about to turn 50, decided to let their two-acre estate in Dallas, complete with pond and swimming pool, go to the dogs.

In 1999, the couple donated their 4,500-square-foot luxury home to the SPCA of Texas. Under the agreement, the seven Pomerance dogs, all of whom were abandoned by previous owners, will continue to live on the estate should anything happen to either husband or wife. Furthermore, the SPCA will provide around-the-clock care and free medical attention for the dogs.

Norman and Diane decided to donate their estate to the SPCA because they wanted someone to look after their dogs. They also wanted to avoid either splitting up the pack, or having to institutionalize any of the dogs.

"The SPCA donation is a source of comfort to us," Diane told the *Dallas Morning News.* "I feel tremendous relief that our babies are entrusted to people who will give them loving care."

If you have pets in your life, hopefully you have learned to spread that love around a little. Maybe you send a check once a year to a local animal rescue group or you serve as a volunteer at an animal shelter, helping to walk dogs or groom cats. Perhaps your role is more prominent, both in terms of time and money. Whether as a donor or volunteer, an ongoing relationship with a rescue group or animal shelter is mutually beneficial. Hopefully, the organization is important to you and a special part of your life.

Should such a connection already exist, you may want to involve the local humane society in any decision you make about the future of your animals. Some shelter programs are developing ambitious estate planning strategies to help pet owners, while also helping themselves. Others are opting for a low-key approach where the emphasis remains on placing animals in new homes.

The good news is that there are more than 4,000 animal shelters currently in operation across the United States. The bad news, warns Nina Berkheiser of the SPCA of Pinellas County in Florida, is that the quality of care at those shelters can vary. "Not all shelters are created equally," she says. "There are some places that have dirt floors. One shelter I read about has an after-hours drop-off that sends the animals down a laundry chute into a holding bin. You certainly want to check out the shelter and walk through it. Pay a surprise visit."

You don't have to sign over your house like the Pomerances did in order to be an asset to a humane society. Most are always short-handed and begging for volunteers. Sign up. Get involved. See how the staff and clients interact. Observe how the animals are treated. Study the organizational mission statement. If everything seems positive, you might feel comfortable trusting this group to help out if your pet outlives you. It is easy enough to draw up a provision in your will to leave your animals in the care of a local humane society. (See "Sample Will Provision for Leaving Pets to an Animal Shelter" in Resources.)

Or you may wish to make a more convincing gesture.

• Include the shelter as a beneficiary in your will.

• Make a gift of stock to the shelter.

• Give your paid-up life insurance policy to the shelter.

• Make the shelter the beneficiary of your retirement plan.

• Make a gift of real estate.

"More people are doing planned giving to humane societies," says Jamie Gaunt of the SPCA of Texas. "It's becoming so much more important to people and, at least for now, they have the money. Those of us in the humane industry are realizing the importance of planned giving and we're becoming more proactive instead of just reactive."

But not all shelters respond the same. There is a richness of opinion among humane professionals as to their responsibility in caring for your animals, and your responsibility, as well.

∼

According to the Zimmer Foundation, over 80 percent of the cats who are adopted in this country are placed owner-to-owner, not shelter-to-owner.

∼

The San Francisco SPCA Sido Service

An elderly Bay Area woman lived alone with her dog Sido back in the 1970s. She loved Sido dearly, but feared no one would be around to properly care for the small sheltie mix after the woman died. So she stipulated in her will that, upon her death, the dog was to be put humanely to sleep. The woman died in 1979.

Sido, who was then 11, was placed in the temporary care of the San Francisco SPCA until the will could be probated. However, then SPCA executive director Richard Avanzino and his staff refused to relinquish the dog when the time came for the terms of the will to be carried out.

A huge public outcry followed on behalf of Sido and spilled into the courts in the case of *Smith v. Avanzino* (1980). A judge invalidated the euthanasia provision, concluding that the owner would have wanted her pet to live if a good home could be found. Special legislation was later passed in Sacramento to protect pets like Sido. The dog eventually went to live with a new family and enjoyed another five years of life.

Sido's close call led SPCA officials to establish the Sido Service, which today is free to all San Francisco SPCA members. *If something happens to a pet owner, the Sido Service guarantees placement of the healthy pet in a new home, as well as regular medical care in the society's animal hospital.* Staff members also check in periodically with the new owners to ensure that all is well. There is a limit of two pets per household. Age is not a factor, but the animals must be in good health and free of serious behavior problems.

The program certainly made a difference for Samantha, an eight-year-old German shepherd mix, and Trilby, a fourteen-year-old retriever mix. Nicknamed the "Golden Girls," they were the companion animals of Arthur, who died in his late seventies shortly after enrolling both dogs in the Sido Service. The San Francisco SPCA was able to step in and care for the dogs, eventually finding a new family who wanted both Samantha and Trilby. (See Resources for Sido Service contact information.)

Seattle Animal Control

Over the years a traditional tug of war about how to care for animals has taken place in communities across the country. On one end, are the city or county departments involved with animal control; on the other end are the humane shelters and volunteers dedicated to animal rescue. The tugging can get quite fierce when opposing philosophies clash.

Then there is the curious case of Seattle Animal Control, a large city agency blessed with a vast volunteer network and an ambitious planned giving program that rivals anything being done by nonprofit humane societies. Yes, they have a mandate for animal control, but manager Don Jordan insists he has a heart to match his brain. "We used to be the outlaw in the community. Nobody liked us," he admits. "We had such a poor image. So we opened the program up to the community and allowed them to participate in twenty different volunteer opportunities. Today we've got six hundred volunteers and a great networking system throughout the community."

Jordan, who took over the department in 1996, fields phone calls regularly from his counterparts in the public sector around the country who are all trying to figure out how Jordan works his magic. In truth, the impetus dates back to 1977 when the city of Seattle established a Help the Animals Fund, allowing Animal Control to receive gifts and donations from the public for the purpose of promoting animal welfare.

"Because we have this fund set up, it's separate from the city budget and tax-exempt under the IRS code, even though we're a government agency," explains Jordan. "Because we get this money, we can offer programs we wouldn't be able to otherwise." Jordan figures his department spends $100,000 annually just on veterinary bills to help sick animals recover. Most animal control facilities would just euthanize and save the money.

But Jordan has learned to think creatively. He is especially proud of one pet program, "Get Fit With Fido," where runners come by and check out dogs for daily jogs. Another program, which promotes planned giving, has enjoyed some initial success in the last two years, including bequests to Animal Control from area residents in the amounts of $45,000, $95,000, and $245,000.

Jordan is busy spreading the word that his department will now step in and help find new homes for animals after the owners have died. If you name Seattle Animal Control in your will or other deferred giving arrangement, the organization will take custody of your animals when the time comes.

"We want people to include us in their wills, yes," says Jordan. "But we'll do it regardless. We won't turn anyone down. I personally know of dozens and dozens of cases where people have passed away and a family member has relinquished the pet to us. The family is distraught and they simply can't care for the animal. A lot of pet owners don't plan ahead. They're not in the mindset to include their pets in their wills. So the last stop is us."

People living outside Seattle need to make arrangements to have their pets transported to Animal Control if they want to take advantage of Jordan's offer. But they won't stay long at the facility; Animal Control tries to get pets in foster homes as quickly as possible. "We want them out of the shelter environment because of all the stress," says Jordan. "They've just lost their owners and now have probably gone to two or three stops before coming to us. We'll put them on the Internet and work the adoption process. We will never turn away an animal." (See Resources for Seattle Animal Control contact information.)

SPCA of Texas

Jamie Gaunt serves as planned giving manager for the SPCA of Texas, based in Dallas. Although she has only been on the job for less than a year, Jamie has already accumulated a lifetime of chilling memories. "We see a lot of old dogs and cats come in. They're older animals and most families don't want the Chihuahua with only one tooth left and shaking all over. This work can break your heart sometimes."

Gaunt is proud of the success enjoyed by the SPCA of Texas,

but she understands that there are always more animals in need, particularly from pet owners who have died without taking the time to plan carefully for their animals. This is Gaunt's specialty. She believes the role of the animal shelter is to provide guidance to clients and outline their options about long-term planning.

"People really need advice about what to do in terms of estate planning," Gaunt says. "But I can only do so much because of liability issues. One of my main jobs is to reassure these people who call in that they're not crazy when they say, 'I know this may sound crazy, but I want to figure out something to do with my animals if something happens to me.' They're not silly at all. I act as a buffer and try to connect them with a professional financial planner."

Even though Texas has not passed pet trust legislation, twenty-eight families bequeathed a total of $4,445,000 to the SPCA between 1996 and 1999, all of it through wills, insurance policies, and trusts to assure a future for their animal companions. Florence Krol of Dallas, for example, recently left $75,000 to the SPCA of Texas to care for her three cats Mishka, Nickolai, and Alexi should they outlive her.

The SPCA of Texas offers perpetual care through the Pet Survivor Life Care program. For a minimum donation of $10,000, your pet will be placed with a new family and be given free lifetime healthcare through the SPCA veterinary staff. The organization makes regular follow-up visits to assure that the pets are adjusting well to their new environment. However, Gaunt is quick to point out that there is some flexibility to this part of the program; actually an estate gift in any amount assures that the SPCA will find a new home for your animal.

"Some people tell us they can't afford $10,000 per pet," says Gaunt. "I tell them, 'Look, just put us in your will. I want you to be comfortable.' I'd rather have that than face family members who want to euthanize animals."

The other part of the program requires a minimum gift of

$25,000 for a small animal (dog, cat, bird), or $50,000 for a large animal (horse, donkey, llama). Sign on the dotted line and your pet gets to move into the SPCA Life Care Cottage, a three-bedroom house located on a large parcel of land in suburban Dallas.

The acreage and house were purchased through a $270,000 donation from the Dealey family of Dallas; there is room on the property for additional cottages if future demand warrants. Pets have indoor access to the living room and doggie den or kitty playroom; there are also extensive outside areas for exercise, all under staff supervision. No cages are used.

Gaunt currently has a waiting list of forty-three cats and twenty-one dogs who will eventually move into the cottage if their owners die or become incapacitated. Why keep them in a cottage? Why not just find new homes for all the animals? It's not that simple, says Gaunt. "Some people are so particular about their cats or dogs or horses that they don't want them in another house, with another family. We have plenty of people who tell us, 'Oh, our kitties can't go to anybody else.' So either they're euthanized or they come here." (See Resources for SPCA of Texas contact information.)

Marin Humane Society

Diane Allevato has seen a lot of needless pain and suffering in the twenty-one years that she has been involved with the Marin Humane Society in Northern California. Currently serving as executive director, Allevato still sounds frustrated as she describes what happens far too often when pets outlive their humans.

"We see tragedy here at least every week," she begins. "An older person dies without making provisions for the dog, cat, guinea pig, or bird. The family—and that's under the best of circumstances, that there is a family—sweeps into town. The family, well, they all love Mom, but they don't love her dog. Or Mom had twelve cats and no one wants to deal with it, so off to the shelter they go."

Allevato explains that this is the worst of circumstances. "First, the animals are traumatized because they're confused. Second, we don't know anything about the animals. And neither does the son or daughter because they've been living on the East Coast for twenty years. So we constantly end up with animals that we know nothing about."

To try and stay ahead of the game, Allevato started the Guardians for Life program in 1991. She wanted to try and get as much information about individual animals on file before the owner died. Allevato also wanted to offer Guardians for Life as a way of thanking humane society members for their support. This is a wonderful win-win program: "You help us now, we'll help you later."

The concept is relatively simple. No donation is required to enroll in Guardians for Life, but you have to be a member of the Marin Humane Society; anyone can join for $25 per year. Nor is there a limit on the number of pets you can include, but extensive paperwork is requested for each animal. "We want people to tell us everything," Allevato says. "We want to know what the dog's favorite toy is and which animals get along together and what type of medication they might need." Computer-generated postcards are sent out every eighteen months to remind people to update their pet information.

When you die, or become incapacitated, shelter volunteers come to your house and take custody of all companion animals. They are kept at the shelter or in foster homes until new adoption arrangements can be made. Shelter officials strive to honor any requests you might make about your animal companions' future, but final placement decisions are up to them.

This program is very successful. According to Allevato, the program enjoys a perfect adoption record. "During the ten years of Guardians for Life, we've never been unable to place an orphan. We have a 100 percent success rate." The reason, she says, is the strong animal-friendly ethic embraced by the Marin County community, just north of San Francisco. "We try not to keep the orphans in the shelter very long," explains Allevato. "We'll try to market them for the qualities they have. In order for it to all come together, you need three things: a strong network of foster homes, a shelter in a position to make these animals visible and a newsletter or Web access to find good homes. Our program really depends on the goodwill of the community."

The Marin Humane Society often gets large donations from people with the caveat that they want their pets taken in by the shelter once the owners have died. Allevato says that she doesn't particularly like that approach because it implies that only people who can donate large amounts of money will be able to have their pets cared for. "You don't have to give us money. We'll do the right thing," she insists. "If you have six cats, you don't have to give us $60,000. We'll take them all in and do everything we possibly can."

Still, despite the impressive success, Allevato is the first to admit that Guardians for Life is not the best solution for what happens when your pet outlives you. To her, that's what friends are for. "The ideal thing really is a friend or family member who loves your dog, or cat, or bird, or horse, as much as you do. and accepts that responsibility not as a burden but as a gesture of love." (See Resources for Marin Humane Society contact information.)

SPCA of Pinellas County

Nina Berkheiser hears the question all the time. "What if..." as in "What if I donated $100,000 to your shelter? Would you take care of my pet for life if something happened to me?"

The answer, surprisingly, is no. While some would jump at the offer, Berkheiser, who serves as development director for the SPCA of Pinellas County, Florida, believes such an arrangement is counterproductive to the mission of her animal shelter.

"No, we don't provide that service because what they're really talking about is putting an animal in a cage for another five or six years and that is in direct violation of our mission. We believe that these are companion animals and as such, they need to be in homes with companions. We start from that premise."

This SPCA is too busy to worry about perpetual care; they're more focused on the plight of 17,000 animals in the Tampa-St. Petersburg area. It can be an uphill battle. In 1999, there were 77,000 dogs and cats turned over to area shelters. More than 23,000 were claimed by owners or adopted, but the other 49,000 were euthanized.

The state of Florida has yet to pass specific pet trust legislation, but they do have a tough animal control ordinance on the books. By law, the continued abandonment of a pet for ten days after written notice to the owner authorizes the pet to be delivered to the nearest humane society or county animal control. The statute further mandates that abandoning an animal means that the owner relinquishes all rights to the pet.

Berkheiser and her colleagues face an additional challenge because of the significant senior population in her state, elderly people whose only real friend may be a pet. "You have senior citizens who tell their attorney, 'I want all my animals euthanized.' These pets are their only family and they're positive that no one else will take as good of care of the pets as they did. But if the animal is young and healthy, it's really not fair."

So Berkheiser fights the good fight, focusing her attention on free estate planning seminars for local attorneys and CPAs, stressing how pet owners can legally protect their animals. Her hope is that these professionals, in turn, can educate their clients.

"Here's what I tell people in my seminars. 'You've got two choices. You can ignore the pet issue and deal with it when your client dies—guess who's going to get stuck with that cat? Or you can be proactive and deal with it up front.' My sense is that we've been able to raise their consciousness a little on this issue. They're starting to pay attention."

Asked about the role of the animal shelter in this process, Berkheiser suggested a more important question that should be driving the entire humane effort: *What is best for the animal?*

"This is what it all comes down to with any decision regarding pets. Can you truly say that what you're doing is really what's best for the animal? An animal shelter should be a fallback position. We provide a safety net if everything else falls through. Find a friend who understands the commitment to your pets and is willing to do it. Then find a back-up friend. Put it all down in your estate plan. If your two friends fall through, then put in the name of the animal shelter you want to use. But be specific about which shelter—you don't want them going to animal control." (See Resources for SPCA of Pinellas County contact information.)

TEN

Veterinarians and Veterinary Schools

New Englanders Diane and Mark were blessed to have Eric, a beautiful and friendly golden retriever. They adopted Eric as a puppy ten years ago, but Diane was the first to admit that this was Mark's dog. Eric wanted to be wherever Mark was. They played together constantly. If Mark fell asleep on the couch, Eric would leap up and lie down next to him. He would carry around Mark's shoes or a pair of his socks all day. To Diane, Eric was simply a loving and devoted dog.

Then in January 2000, Mark died during a house fire. Eric was outside at the time and Diane was away. Firefighters tried to grab the dog, but in all the confusion and excitement, Eric ran off into the night.

The next morning, a distraught Diane returned to the house, looking for Eric. She found the dog—lying on the couch, even though it was burned out. He was there, waiting for Mark, because this was their special place together. Seeing Eric stretched out on the fire-ravaged couch only compounded Diane's grief.

Diane did not know what to do. She couldn't keep Eric—it

would be too painful to have her late husband's dog around. Friend after friend said no to adopting Eric. They all had their excuses. Diane thought briefly about euthanizing the dog, but quickly realized that was not an acceptable option. In desperation, she turned to their veterinarian and pleaded for assistance. Having been in this situation before, the veterinarian was able to put Diane in touch with Yankee Golden Retriever Rescue of Massachusetts. The rescue group agreed to take Eric and find him a new home.

The Role of the Veterinarian

Comprehensive planning for your pet demands some type of support system, whether it is a close friend volunteering to be a caretaker, a seasoned attorney representing you in court, or a respected humane society finding a new home for your tabby cat. You are going to turn to one, or all, of these sources to help protect your companion animals. There is another person for you to consider as part of this mix—your veterinarian, a likely person to know first-hand how much your pets mean to you. Veterinarians are typically involved in major birth-through-death decisions made by pet owners. Whether you end up with a detailed pet trust, or a simple caretaker arrangement, involve your veterinarian in your final decision.

Jean Hofve, a Denver veterinarian, believes her colleagues will be receptive to the discussion. "Practitioners are getting more and more involved in this question," says Dr. Hofve. "I think a comparison can be made to pet loss. Ten years ago, there was very little discussion about pet loss in our field. Today, the whole veterinary profession is becoming more cognizant of the human-animal bond, the need to nurture that bond, as well as the need to provide options when the bond breaks down, for whatever reason. If clients are concerned about what will happen to their pets, they should ask their vets. The faster the client asks, the faster vets come up to speed."

A veterinarian can be a strong resource on any number of different levels. First, the average practitioner has considerable experience in placing unwanted animals in new homes. Far too often veterinary clinics serve as dumping grounds for abandoned cats, dogs, and parrots who wind up on clinic front porches and behind trash cans. Your veterinarian may know another client looking to adopt a specific animal.

In addition, your veterinarian may be aware of options that may be unfamiliar to you. Dr. Hofve regularly refers her clients to a long-term cat center in Denver, a facility mostly unknown to the average pet owner. "It doesn't hurt to talk things over with your vet and see what your options are," she advises. "Your vet might know more than you suspect."

Julie Weiss Murad of The Gabriel Foundation echoes the same sentiment. "Veterinarians can be invaluable because they are able to evaluate protocol and can help clients formulate key questions to ask. A lot of these programs are well known to veterinarians. After all, vets are a small network. They keep in contact and they're well aware that there are some treacherous situations out there."

Perhaps most importantly, if your veterinarian is involved in this decision, you will keep the cycle of pet care going. If you opt for the pet trust route, both your trustee and your caretaker should meet with your veterinarian to facilitate the transition. Anyone who is going to eventually be responsible for your pets should know, and be known by, the veterinarian involved.

A Veterinary Pet Care Contract

Another way to directly involve your veterinarian is to create a veterinary pet care contract (see Sample Veterinary Pet Care Contract on page 137). Let's face it: anyone who steps in to care for your animals is going to be hit with medical bills. The cost of vaccinations, check-ups, and medical emergencies add up over time.

You can help ease the financial burden somewhat by making a financial arrangement with your veterinarian in advance. Agree to a certain sum of money that will be used to cover future veterinary expenses, thus lifting that burden off the caretaker. Work out an arrangement so that the cycle of pet care continues unbroken; a contract is an ideal way of reaching that goal.

Dr. Hofve encourages people to set aside money now and speak with their veterinarians. "It's nice to provide financial care for the animal, even part of the cost. You're asking someone else to assist in the care of your animals. That could be eighteen or twenty years."

The Veterinary School Care Option

Lately, veterinary schools have begun to offer a totally new option for pet owners to consider. An article in the *San Antonio Business Journal* caught our attention when it described how one retired couple decided to provide for their only cat. Concerned about what might happen after they died, the couple enrolled in a special program offered by Texas A&M University. In exchange for a $25,000 donation to the veterinary school, the university agreed to pick up the cat after the couple died and provide all medical needs and day-to-day care for the rest of the cat's life.

Offering long-term shelter for companion animals is a concept that a handful of veterinary schools are beginning to explore; most programs have been functioning for less than a decade. Purdue University began its Peace of Mind program in 1994 after an Evansville woman contacted the veterinary school and asked officials to set up a program for her dog. Within two years, more than a dozen animals had been placed in Peace of Mind—dogs, cats, parrots, and horses—each getting lifetime care in return for a $25,000 donation to Purdue.

The University of Florida, Sun City Center has announced

plans to build a five-acre, $3 million center to house animals who have outlived their owners. Donations will cover the cost of construction. Plans call for separate common areas for cats and dogs that include upholstered furniture, carpeting, and a TV set.

Every veterinary care program is different, but the underlying principle seems to be the same: the pet needs a good home, the university always needs money, let's get together. Advocates push veterinary centers as a win-win situation. The animal companion receives plenty of attention and first-rate medical care. Meanwhile, the university benefits from major donations, and veterinary students get a chance to practice their "patient skills" by interacting with animals in a loving, home-like environment. Some programs offer the animals up for adoption, while others keep them on campus for life.

You do not have to be a graduate of a particular university to affiliate with its program. Here are some of the more established long-term veterinary pet care centers.

Kansas State University

If you'll take Manhattan for your pet, Kansas State University (KSU) might be worth investigating. Located in Manhattan, Kansas, KSU offers the Perpetual Pet Care Program through its College of Veterinary Medicine. The arrangement is relatively simple—you agree to set up an endowed scholarship for a KSU veterinary student. In turn, if something happens to you, that student takes your pet and promises to love and care for the animal. Unlike other university programs, there is no specific housing at KSU for the pet. The student takes the pet home to live.

The veterinary student can qualify for the program only by being in good academic standing and expressing an interest in a particular animal. Applicants are carefully screened by the veterinary school before being awarded the scholarship.

Pet owners, meanwhile, may specify the type of food and

housing they want their animal companions to have, as well as the amount of daily exercise. Comprehensive medical care is provided through the veterinary hospital. A detailed contract also spells out what will happen to the pet after the veterinary student graduates. Some animals stay with their student owners; others are re-assigned to new students. (See Resources for contact information.)

The minimum gifts to enroll in the KSU program per animal are:

- Small companion animal – $25,000
- Large companion animal – $50,000
- Special need – $75,000

Texas A&M University

If Texas hospitality sounds more appealing, then head for College Station, home of Texas A&M University. The Stevenson Companion Animal Life-Care Center was established by the Texas A&M College of Veterinary Medicine in 1993, the vision of E.W. Ellet, DVM, former head of the Small Animal Clinic. Ellet's dream was made possible through a generous donation from Madlin Stevenson, a life-long animal lover who died in 2000. Her five cats, seven dogs, one pony, and a llama currently reside at the center.

Stevenson Center clients include pet owners who are about to enter a retirement home, as well as those who may be hospitalized for an extended period of time. But most of the clients are people who want to make sure in advance that their pets will be cared for. In addition, these are people who have the financial means to place their animal companions at the Stevenson Center. Typically a bed at the Stevenson Center costs between $50,000 and $100,000 per animal. Less expensive options are available, depending upon how far in advance you enroll, but the minimum is $10,000.

What does all that money buy? A lifetime of healthy food

and free medical care, for starters. An experienced veterinary technician is on staff and several Texas A&M veterinary students live on-site to help care for the animals. The 5,000-square-foot residential facility, located on the Texas A&M campus, is made to look and feel just like home. It is directly adjacent to the veterinary school and there are plans to add an additional 3,500 square feet.

Pets at the Stevenson Center live in an open environment and are free to roam the premises. Unlike the Kansas State program, these four-legged residents are not eligible for adoption. Today, about twenty-five pets reside at the facility and several hundred pet owners across the country have already paid $1,000 ($2,000 for a large pet) to reserve a place for their animals at Texas A&M. (See Resources for contact information.)

Oklahoma State University

Oklahoma might be OK with your dog or cat after you've gone. Oklahoma State University (OSU) in Stillwater is home to the Cohn Family Shelter for Small Animals, which opened in 1998.

The goal was to take the eight acres just north of the university veterinary hospital and transform it into a comfortable home-like setting for small and large animals alike. Features of the Cohn Family Shelter include outdoor runs and separate kennels, grooming and examination areas, a giant pet playroom, and live-in apartments for staff to provide twenty-four-hour observation and care. An on-site veterinarian assures that each animal will have complete access to full medical care.

In addition, OSU veterinary students provide much of the pet care. The Cohn Family Shelter provides a unique pedagogical opportunity to observe and interact with companion animals, offering tender and loving long-term care to the animals. As with the Texas A&M program, these pets are not available for adoption.

Meanwhile, money derived from the Cohn Family Shelter

program funds the OSU veterinary school. The minimum gifts to enroll in the Oklahoma State program per animal are:

- Cat – $15,000
- Dog – $25,000
- Large animal – $50,000

A 5 percent non-refundable reservation fee is required at the time of application. (See Resources for contact information.)

Before You Enroll

Judging by the enrollment numbers, many pet owners are satisfied with arranging for a veterinary school to care for their companion animals. Others, however, are likely to balk over the relatively high cost of endowment—anywhere from $15,000 to $100,000 per animal. Many pet owners, especially those with multiple animals, simply cannot afford that degree of financial commitment.

In addition to financial considerations, there are other basic questions you need to ask before enrolling your pet in a veterinary school program (see Checklist for Prospective Veterinary School Pet Centers on page 111). Once your questions have been answered, be sure to get everything in writing. Have your attorney sign off on any written agreement. Given the strong academic reputation of the schools involved, there is little doubt that your pet would receive excellent medical care under these programs.

At the same time, you have to consider what is best for your animal companion. Do you want your pet sent off to live in an expensive, long-term care facility with dozens of other animals, or would you prefer seeing Tanner and Jaybird end up in a private home as part of a new family environment? How you answer that question is a good indicator of how seriously you should investigate the veterinary school placement option.

Checklist for Prospective Veterinary School Pet Centers

Before your sign your pet over to the care of a veterinary school center, ask a few basic questions. Any responsible program should be happy to answer the following:

• What type of food are the pets fed and how often?

• Does the program allow for special dietary needs?

• Does the program accept pets regardless of age and medical needs?

• What is the skill level of veterinary care provided?

• Is it staff or students providing the medical treatment?

• How long has the program existed?

• What type of exercise do the pets receive?

• What kind of human contact do the pets receive?

• Are the animals left in cages, or are they allowed to roam free?

• Does the program allow for specific burial wishes?

• What happens to the pets if the facility ceases to exist?

• Are the pets ever eligible for adoption by outside families?

• What happens to the pet after the student caretaker graduates?

• Are other clients available to be interviewed?

• How much money must be paid in advance before a pet is accepted?

Eleven

Pet Retirement Homes
and Sanctuaries

Linda East, DVM, had a problem. Actually the Denver veterinarian had two problems—a pair of older felines named Mrs. Anderson and Mrs. Blake. She had originally rescued the cats as strays several years before and eventually placed both of them with a client, a young woman who fell instantly for both animals. The three lived together happily for the next seven years.

Then the woman died unexpectedly with no provisions for the cats so Mrs. Anderson and Mrs. Blake, now much older, came back to Dr. East. The goal was to keep the cats together, but placing older animals can be difficult, if not impossible. Further complicating matters was the extreme shyness of Mrs. Blake. Dr. East had to think outside the box and devise a nontraditional adoption. Where could these cats go together and be safe? The Whole Cat Store and its owner Sue Green came to mind.

The south Denver store is an emporium of feline natural food and holistic remedies. Green had never had a store cat before. Dr. East convinced her that she needed two. Mrs. Anderson and Mrs. Blake retired to The Whole Cat Store where they continue to live full-time. There was a slight adjustment period for the two cats, but things have worked out. Mrs. Blake parades up and down the aisles, actively seeking attention from customers. Mrs. Anderson pens a regular column for the store's newsletter.

Mrs. Blake and Mrs. Anderson are two of the lucky ones. They bask in the royal treatment that many animals unfortunately will never know. Few stores or offices allow pets on the premises, despite research that demonstrates how beneficial animals in the workplace can be. It's a wonderful idea, but not a realistic option for the majority of animals seeking new homes.

There is, however, a dramatic surge in the opening of pet retirement homes or pet sanctuaries across the United States and Canada, a significant number just in the last five years. From Boston to San Diego, individuals and organizations have opened their doors, offering to provide lifelong care for dogs, cats, horses, reptiles, parrots, goats, whatever, after you die. A few ambitious groups are even considering setting up a nationwide chain of retirement centers.

The concept of a pet retirement home mirrors its human counterpart (see Resources for more information). In exchange for a set fee, your animals are taken in and given shelter, exercise, medical care, and food—all that is missing is the bingo game. And like human retirement homes, some of the pet programs are of a higher quality than others. Pet owners beware.

"Pet retirement homes represent a new trend in pet care," says Lisa Micallef, who runs the Home for Life pet retirement center in Wisconsin. "It's the direct result of the baby boomers and their love for animals. I think it's a very exciting option."

Take your choice. There's Kitty City in New Jersey, Last Chance for Life in Oklahoma, and the Bide-A-Wee Golden Years Retirement Home in New York. To give you a better idea of how the concept works, here are snapshots of three pet retirement centers currently in operation.

The Wild Cat Ranch

Paula Blankenhorn swears that it is just a happy coincidence that her pet retirement home, the Wild Cat Ranch, is located in Comfort, Texas. But that's exactly what the ex-IBM project manager tries to offer 365 days of the year—comfort for her animal guests, and especially for those humans who are worried about what will eventually happen to their companion animals.

Located about sixty-five miles southwest of Austin, the sprawling Wild Cat Ranch is currently home to 162 cats, 7 dogs, and 6 potbellied pigs. "I'm a soft touch," says Blankenhorn, who someday envisions having as many as six hundred animals on her fifty-three-acre dairy goat ranch. Her animals are not available for adoption. When they come to the hill country of Texas, it's to stay.

Blankenhorn's idea for a pet retirement home became reality back in 1995 when she was working outside Washington, D.C. Her boss had a neighbor who was being relocated to Hong Kong for two years and needed someone to look after two elderly cats. Blankenhorn stepped in and as word of her "new" business spread, more animals were added to her menagerie. By the time she moved to Texas two years later, Blankenhorn had twenty-four cats in her care.

Working with her husband Jim, Blankenhorn converted an old forty-foot by thirty-two-foot horse barn into a cattery. There are no cages at Wild Cat Ranch; cats have free run of the barn and access to screened outside porches. The climate-controlled barn interior is carpeted, furnished, and complete with large picture windows for extra sunlight. The cats wander among various scratching posts and old pine tree trunks, chasing each other up and down the long walkways or playing with a mountain of toys.

There are separate areas for cats with AIDS or feline leukemia. Each cat is combed once a week, vaccinated annually, and receives dental care every two years. Volunteers clean and disinfect the area daily and make sure that each cat has some level of human interaction. There have been no outbreaks of disease among the cats since Blankenhorn opened her operation.

The feline residents of the ranch come from all over the country, their owners drawn to Blankenhorn by her compassion and very reasonable rates. "I'm cheap. I'm good. And I care about the animals," is her explanation.

Wild Cat Ranch only charges what it costs to maintain and care for the animals. Basic expenses for each cat include food, kitty litter, insurance, electricity, cleaning solutions, cleaning labor, and emergency medical supplies. The monthly fee is about $100. For multiple pets from one family, the fee is discounted on a sliding scale; 50 percent less for the second pet, 66 percent less for the third, and a 75 percent discount for all additional pets. If you have four cats, for example, your monthly fee is $210 per month. If paid in advance, the twelfth month is free.

"Owners pay us what they can afford," Blankenhorn says. "We will never turn away an animal in need. We often end up dealing with elderly clients on fixed incomes who worry that after they die, their family members will just shoot their cats to be rid of them. We're willing to work with people in order to save the cats."

Wild Cat Ranch accepts dogs, cats, horses, mules, donkeys, goats, and potbellied pigs on a temporary basis if you have an emergency situation or become incapacitated. You can also instruct your veterinarian to send your pets, with proper health certificates, to Wild Cat in the event of your death. Blankenhorn has made arrangements with Austin attorney Brenda Freeman to provide legal forms and assistance in setting up a trust for a modest fee.

"Some people purchase a life insurance policy and name us as a beneficiary, or set up a trust fund through their banks," Blankenhorn says. "But most of our clients set up a will naming us as the beneficiary of a flat fee to pay for their pets' care." (See Resources for contact information.)

The Gabriel Foundation

Julie Weiss Murad has a passion for parrots. She established The Gabriel Foundation to honor her cherished hyacinth macaw who died at twenty-two months old due to lack of a proper medical diagnosis. Under Murad's leadership, The Gabriel Foundation has achieved national recognition for its work in parrot rescue and education programs. An important component for the sanctuary, currently home to 150 parrots, is the Lifetime of Love option.

Parrot owners are invited to bequeath their birds to The Gabriel Foundation upon the owner's death or disability. Murad has fought to keep program costs down. She is concerned that typically only people with lots of money can afford long-term care for their parrots. "What about the person who loves a bird, but dies with only $100 in a checking account? Doesn't that bird deserve to be cared for, as well?" she asks.

People can designate The Gabriel Foundation as a beneficiary on their life insurance policies, retirement accounts, or pension plans. The size of the bequest needed to enroll your parrot in the Lifetime of Love program varies with the breed of the bird. A finch or canary costs $90 per year, while a cockatiel is more expensive at $150 per year. The highest fee is reserved for either a macaw or a cockatoo, which costs $600 annually.

Gabriel fees are inexpensive compared to some other animal sanctuaries, Murad insists. In return, the parrots are cared for by a trained staff of five; each bird is personally handled at least twice daily. A Certified Veterinary Technician is kept on staff and the birds take advantage of an 8,500-square-foot aviary complete with inside play areas and outdoor flights. All animals are regularly examined by an avian veterinarian and the staff makes sure the birds have a nutritious, well-balanced diet.

Birds who come into the Lifetime of Love program are eligible for adoption unless the owner requests otherwise. People looking to adopt parrots from The Gabriel Foundation are subject to a highly structured committee screening process and all birds are tracked annually once they leave the refuge. "Some birds miss being in a home situation," explains Murad. "If birds have had the pleasure and enrichment of living in a home, is it fair to leave them without a lot of intensive interaction? That's why we will adopt out under certain conditions. We want to do what's best for the bird."

Murad eventually would like to set up a series of small bird sanctuaries across the country, based on her Aspen facility, each one handling no more than 150 birds. "There simply aren't enough facilities to care for all the parrots in this country," explains Murad. "They are suffering enormously." (See Resources for contact information.)

∼

Most parrot rescue groups handle between fifty and one hundred birds annually. The largest groups report receiving three hundred or more each year.

∼

Home for Life Animal Sanctuary

Lisa Micallef remembers being a volunteer at the local animal shelter in St. Paul, Minnesota when she was only eight years old. A lot of dogs and cats never made it out alive. Being exposed to such regular euthanasia definitely made an impression on the young girl. Micallef grew up to become an attorney in the Twin Cities, but she never forgot the animals. First came the volunteer legal work on behalf of local humane groups. Then Micallef gradually accumulated her own animal family, including three cats, two dogs and six parrots.

But then she kept encountering animals belonging to elderly

people or people with AIDS. Once the owner died, no family member wanted the animals. Micallef decided it was time to do something, so she opened the Home for Life sanctuary in 1997 on forty acres of land in Star Prairie, Wisconsin, about an hour east of the Twin Cities.

The 180 dogs and cats currently living in Star Prairie are cared for on a 24/7 basis by a staff of ten. There are no cages on the premises. Cats are housed in compatible groups in airy and open catteries. Dogs enjoy separate kennels with outdoor runs; larger fenced-in areas are nearby for the dogs to run and exercise.

Inside the main building, there is a grooming salon, a kitchen for food preparation, sterilizing unit for food dishes, a laundry room, and extensive storage area. Local veterinarians and groomers care for the animals as needed. The Wisconsin facility is a prototype for what Micallef hopes will eventually become a nationwide network of pet retirement homes. "I think our program is both unique and innovative," says Micallef. "Most animal facilities aren't designed nor intended for long-term care, so there's a different emphasis when it comes to staffing and space usage."

A special branch of Home for Life is the AngelCare program, specifically targeted for the mature pet owner age 50 through 79. Anyone can enroll in the program, but the cost, like standard insurance, varies with age. For example, a pet owner between 40 and 49 years old could enroll a dog in AngelCare for $500. That same dog belonging to a person over 70 would cost $1,700. In return, Home for Life agrees to provide lifetime care for a pet when the owner dies. None of the animals are available for adoption.

"One of the problems with most pet sanctuaries is cost. They're just so expensive. Few people can afford them," says Micallef. "What we've tried to do is establish a great place and keep it realistic so that our monthly budget remains within reach."

Micallef has taken out a series of large life insurance policies to protect the Home for Life animals should something happen to her. She worries, though, about the elderly and what will happen to their pets.

"Our seniors seem to have become more and more isolated. They're so much more attached to their pets today. These animals mean literally everything to them and they just worry so much about what will happen to their pets. We're only trying to get people, especially the elderly, to plan ahead so that their pets will have a safe place to go." (See Resources for contact information.)

Considering the Pet Retirement Home Option

On paper, it all sounds pretty good. Put some money down and your pet will be pampered for life. Most of the retirement homes are considerably cheaper than similar programs offered through veterinary schools. And the responsible facilities provide equal doses of love and quality care for your companion animals. For pet owners without sympathetic family members or friends, the retirement home option, if affordable, may be worth pursuing.

Be sure to consult with your veterinarian. This is a decision that requires thorough investigation, according to Deborah Elliott, president of Furr Angels, a Tennessee animal rescue group. Elliott worries that all too often humans fail to plan adequately for their animal companions. Critical decisions are rushed. If you want to consider bequeathing your animal to a pet retirement center, Elliott urges you to ask critical questions in advance. (See "Checklist for Prospective Pet Retirement Homes" on page 123.) "It's so important to get answers up front," Elliott advises. "Many of these retirement homes are relatively new. You need to find out as much as you can about the quality of life your animal will experience."

A key question to consider when researching retirement homes is the financial stability of the facility. How many of these retirement homes will still be in operation five, ten, or fifteen years from now? Is this the future of pet care, or just a passing fancy? If you send your three cats off to live in North Carolina and the operation folds two years later, what happens to your animals?

Criticism of pet retirement homes by some can be harsh. "We all know what it's like to put grandma in one of those places," argues one shelter manager. "Do we really want to put our cats there? It's not home. Home is a home. A retirement center is a retirement center. Decisions need to be made that speak to an individual animal."

Nancy Peterson of The Humane Society of the United States has been especially vocal on the subject. She is worried about the impact such a "warehouse environment" may have on pets who have lived for years as part of a household.

"Our cats and dogs are called companion animals and that's not just because we need them," says Peterson. "They need us, those pets who have lived in a home, have been beloved family members. If they go to a long-term care facility, I doubt that they're really going to get the same quality care and attention that they would get in someone's home."

Peterson is wary of what she calls "Mom and Pop places," retirement centers operating purely on the goodness of the human heart, but not always blessed with the financial know-how to survive. Like Elliott, she urges prospective customers to ask the tough questions. "What's the financial status of this place? Will they be around in a few years? Are they going to run into problems? Caring for animals on a massive scale is much more complicated than a lot of people realize. And it costs a lot of money, too. Things could change at the drop of a hat."

Owners of retirement homes believe they've made a difference for thousands of animals who otherwise wouldn't be alive today. They are driven by passion, not by profit. Back on the Wild Cat Ranch, Paula Blankenhorn, who is anything but retiring, has heard all the criticism before. She doesn't buy it. "Our retirement center has furniture, we have rugs. I'm in there most of the day—

twelve, fourteen hours at a time—walking around, petting and interacting with each cat. They come and jump on my shoulders. It's a completely home-like environment here. And if something happens to me, then the board of directors steps in to keep things going." A bit exasperated, Blankenhorn concludes, "Look, if someone has a better idea, I'd like to hear it."

Almost all the pet retirement homes maintain fairly detailed websites about their programs. Visit the website. Even better, go visit the people and take a walk around the facility. See for yourself how the animals are being treated and decide if you could imagine your own pets being happy in such an environment.

Checklist for Prospective Pet Retirement Homes

Before you sign your companion animal over to a pet retirement home, don't be reluctant to ask a few basic questions. Any responsible program should be happy to answer the following:

- How long has the facility been in business?
- Is the facility licensed by the state?
- How large is the facility's endowment?
- How large is the staff and what is their background?
- What will happen to the animals should the facility cease to operate?
- Are the animals eligible for adoption? If yes, under what criteria?
- What kind of animal placement rate does the facility have?
- What is the cost per animal? What does that cover?
- What type of food are the pets fed and how often?
- Does the facility allow for special dietary needs?
- Does the facility accept pets regardless of age and medical needs?
- What is the quality of veterinary care provided?
- What type of exercise do the pets receive?
- What kind of human contact do the pets receive?
- Are the pets left in cages, or does the program allow free roaming?
- Does the facility allow for specific burial wishes?

TWELVE

September 11th: The Pets of Ground Zero

We thought we were finished with the manuscript. We thought we had told you everything you needed to know about what happens when your pet outlives you. Then along came September 11, 2001 and we were painfully reminded that there are those singularly horrific events outside the human imagination. What unfolded that morning in New York City and Washington, D.C. involved thousands of people, many of whom have companion animals—making this their story, too.

Animal companions were part of September 11th from the beginning. Chantal Vincelli, who was known for her care of stray and unwanted cats, died in the collapse of the World Trade Center and left behind seventeen cats in her Harlem apartment. What animal lover could hold back tears at the report of blind Omar Eduardo Rivera, a worker trapped on the 71st floor of the World Trade Center, being safely escorted to an emergency exit by his guide dog, Dorado? Who could not be awed by the heroics of the determined search-and-rescue dogs brought in from all over the country to scour through the rubble? One search-and-rescue dog found five trapped firefighters; another dog fell five floors—and lived.

But as emergency forces worked to respond to human needs, another group, composed mainly of New York humane societies, recognized that pets—and pet owners—needed specific crisis assistance. "Time is running out," was the public warning issued by ASPCA President Larry Hawk. "Not everyone has a responsive network of caring friends and family. In fact, the more alone people are, the more likely they are to rely on their pets for loving companionship. Hence, these pets are—and still remain—the most at risk."

ASPCA officials estimated that up to eight hundred pets were orphaned, displaced or died as a result of the September 11th terrorist attacks. The ASPCA and New York's Center for Animal Care and Control (CACC) rescued hundreds of animals from evacuated areas, eventually reuniting them with their owners or finding them foster homes. Among the rescued animals were dogs, cats, snakes, geckos, and a Manhattan rat who was a classroom pet at an elementary school near Ground Zero.

Waggin' Tail Doggie Day Care, located a few blocks from the World Trade Center, had one hundred dogs in the building on the morning of September 11th. Given the large number of dogs on site, evacuation was impossible, so staff remained with the dogs throughout the day. Fortunately, not a single dog was injured.

The primary groups involved in the New York animal companion rescue operation were the ASPCA, the CACC, the Suffolk County SPCA and the Humane Society of New York. All four groups participated in the actual rescue of pets stranded in apartments near the World Trade Center and in the Battery Park City complex. Both the ASPCA and the Suffolk County SPCA stationed mobile veterinary units near Ground Zero. In addition, volunteers from People for the Ethical Treatment of Animals (PETA) came by bus from Virginia to pressure city officials to search for missing pets.

"Our teams would go up ten, twenty flights of stairs in the pitch dark because the elevators weren't working," says Doris Meyer of the CACC. "There were cats that didn't want to be found and dogs that didn't want to walk down stairs." One ASPCA officer, Henry Ruiz, walked up 39 flights of stairs in one TriBeCa apartment building to rescue a gecko named Little Dude who was so traumatized that he had shed his skin.

Terri Crisp, director of Emergency Animal Rescue Service (EARS), rushed to New York from Sacramento after the attacks to join in the search for missing animals. "By Thursday, September 20th, the consensus among the rescue groups was that all the animals in the evacuated area had been located and removed from their homes," Crisp says. For her, finding the animals trapped in apartments was the easy part—the larger challenge involved those frightened pets who ran off through shattered windows.

Many of those animals ended up at the Humane Society of New York. They reported more than two hundred animals either being rescued or brought to their facility on East 59th Street since the attacks. In response, the organization set up a network of foster homes for those companion animals needing temporary or permanent relocation.

Among the recovered animals, several needed treatment for dehydration, irritated eyes, respiratory ailments and shock. Most if not all of these problems were treated at no expense to the surviving owners. A cat named Ewok lost an eye from all the dust and smoke. The cost of his surgery was covered by a donation from EARS in Sacramento.

"About 99.9 percent of the rescues had happy endings," says ASPCA spokeswoman Ruth First. "There will always be those animals we don't know about. We're hoping that the family and friends of victims have checked on pets at the homes and have taken care of them."

The first phase of the ASPCA campaign was a huge success. Next, officials concentrated on reports of still-stranded animals and helped displaced residents care for their pets during the transition period.

Rebecca Morris made an eleven-hundred-mile trek from her home in Hazel Green, Alabama to adopt animals orphaned by the September 11th attacks. Instead, she was asked by the ASPCA to help find homes for four large, difficult-to-place dogs, who had been in New York shelters for more than six months. Two of the dogs only had three legs; a third suffered from a badly injured back. "I know these aren't World Trade Center dogs, but that's OK," Morris later told reporters. "Everybody needs to do their part in helping out after this tragedy."

The ASPCA bought full-page advertisements in several New York newspapers asking neighbors and friends of victims to check for stranded pets. They also organized a database of all apartments with known pets in the Ground Zero vicinity.

Meanwhile, TV star Rue McClanahan made a special public appeal to building superintendents in and around New York City and New Jersey to pay particular attention for sounds from dogs and cats and other animals who may have lost their owners on September 11th. "Supers are the ones who know who comes and goes. If someone hasn't been back to their apartment, or if dogs who normally don't bark or whine start doing so, please go in and give water and food and make a call on their behalf," McClanahan urged. A puppy belonging to a single man who died in the World Trade Center attack was found safe the next day in the man's Manhattan apartment building, thanks to the doorman who kept an updated list of all the building's pets.

One Resourceful Cat

Kathleen Ross had mere moments to evacuate her apartment building, located in the shadow of the World Trade Center, on the morning of September 11th. Ross had heard a loud noise and assumed it was a Hollywood movie crew on location. One look out the window changed her mind. Ross had to leave fast, but not without Tweety-Pye, her five-year-old cat with thick gray hair and yellow eyes.

Ross scrambled to get the cat inside her carrier, but Tweety-Pye was too frightened by the noise to leave. Ross tried to grab the cat. The cat bit her. Emergency crews were ordering people to leave. Ross had no choice.

The building survived, but Ross and her neighbors were kept away for the next five days. "All I wanted was my cat," Ross later said. "I kept telling them, 'I want my cat. I've got to see my cat.'" Finally, police officers and humane society volunteers swept through the abandoned building, looking for any animals trapped inside.

A police officer found Tweety-Pye still inside Ross's apartment. When cat and human were later reunited, Ross was amazed to hear the officer's description of what he had found.

Tweety-Pye had managed to pry open the kitchen cabinet where her bag of food was kept. She dragged the bag into the living room and tore it open. There were also scraps of food and water left in the kitchen sink, providing plenty of nourishment.

In addition, perhaps in response to the constant emergency sirens outside, Tweety-Pye pushed open a sliding closet door in the bedroom, dragged a pillow inside, and created a safe nest for herself in a quiet corner.

~

On October 9th, a female cat and her three, two-week-old kittens were found alive in an abandoned restaurant near Ground Zero. The mother was named Hope and her kittens, Flag, Freedom, and Amber. All four animals made a complete recovery.

Being Prepared for an Emergency

As New Yorkers searched for their lost pets, humane society officials reminded pet owners of the need to be prepared for the next emergency. Whether the concern is an earthquake or terrorist attack, pet owners need to be ready.

- If you live alone and have a pet, tell all your friends and neighbors about the animal and who has a key.

- Leave information with the person responsible for your rental property about who can have access to your property in case of an emergency. Without written authority to enter an apartment or home, a rescue worker may not be allowed inside to rescue an animal.

- Make sure you leave sufficient water and dry food out in case you're unable to return home for a day or two.

- Keep dog leashes and cat carriers in an easy-to-find location in case others need to come in and rescue your pets. Also keep veterinarian contact information near your telephone.

- Microchip your dog or cat. If they become frightened and run away, a microchip will make identification easier should they survive a disaster, and you do not.

Dealing with Rumors

From the outset, rumors flew around New York about what was happening to companion animals after the terrorist attacks. There was rampant anxiety concerning pets of those killed in the attacks being left unattended and starving to death. However, according to Doris Meyer of the New York Center for Animal Care and Control, no such pet deaths were confirmed. Some so-called "orphaned pets" were turned into local shelters, but so far, Meyer says, every animal has found an adoptive home.

Then there were persistent Internet rumors, repeated postings urging people to hurry to any New York shelter because pets supposedly were being relinquished in record numbers following September 11th. "Kill rates at these shelters are very high," warned some of the messages. "Officials have no choice because of the large influx of animals."

"The Internet rumor mill has been out of control," says Ruth First of the ASPCA. "Contrary to rumors, New York shelters were not overcrowded with people relinquishing their pets. In fact, adoptions are up following September 11th and relinquishments are down."

What happened at the New York shelters was more like a scene fresh from a Frank Capra movie. People began showing up, one after another, all interested in adoption. "For some New Yorkers, the desire to connect with an animal in need ended up transcending the immediate impact of the events of September 11th," says Pam Nelson, adoption supervisor at the CACC Manhattan shelter. "They're not looking for World Trade Center orphans, because fortunately we hardly have any of those. But they're just suddenly interested in any animals we have."

Broadway producer Robyn Goodman understood this desire to help animals. Goodman admitted that she was feeling depressed and vulnerable as she walked her dog in New York on the Saturday after the attacks. Stopping by a pet supply store, she noticed cats available for adoption. One caught her eye immediately, a seven-month-old black feline with a white stripe extending from his neck to his stomach.

"It's hard for a lot of New Yorkers, because we want to do something to help and there isn't currently a need for more volunteers," says Goodman, who impulsively adopted the cat and named him Rudi in honor of New York's mayor. "This helped me feel like I saved a life."

I Loved Him Before He Even Got Here

Robin and Derek Latour watched the September 11th tragedy unfold on TV from their suburban San Francisco home. In the days that followed, they wanted to do something, anything, to help. Being devoted animal lovers with three cats and two dogs of their own, the couple began to worry about pets now homeless or ownerless. Robin did some research on the Internet and sent an email to the Suffolk County SPCA in New York, offering to adopt a homeless cat or dog.

"I described myself, our house, where we lived, the animals we already had and offered to take anything that they had that needed a home," says Latour. "I wasn't really sure if I would hear from them. San Francisco is so very far away and I figured that people in New York were probably offering to take the animals."

Three weeks later, Latour was surprised to receive a phone call from Herb Kellner, director of the Suffolk County SPCA. If the couple was still interested, Kellner had a cat who needed a home. The organization, Kellner explained, had fielded a number of phone calls from people offering to take in animals, but most had specific preferences. Robin and Derek were one of the few to say, "We'll take anything."

The cat, a twenty-pound tuxedo named Arthur, a.k.a. "Sweet Angel," belonged to New York Fire Captain Marty Egan Jr., who was killed in the collapse of the World Trade Center. Because of severe allergy problems, Egan's mother could not bring Arthur into her house and she asked repeatedly at her son's wake if anyone would adopt the five-year-old cat. No one offered. Family members tried in vain to place the cat. The Suffolk County SPCA finally stepped in to help find a new home for Arthur.

"We tried finding a closer home, but many of the people who volunteered to adopt cats didn't return our phone calls," says Kellner. "Then I remembered Robin's email."

Robin agreed to take the cat sight unseen. "I had no idea

what Arthur looked like except that he was black and white and large," she says. "And sweet, everyone told me that he was a very sweet cat." American Airlines donated a seat, so it was goodbye New York, hello California.

The Latours and a small horde of media greeted Arthur at the airport. When Robin took the cat out of his cage, he melted onto her shoulder and lazily put a paw on her arm. "I loved him before he even got here," says Latour. "As soon as I held him, he became my kitty. He still is. Arthur likes my husband, but he's really my squishy cat. We had an instant bond."

Derek's grandfather was a fire captain in San Francisco, so adopting the cat of a New York City firefighter gave a special heartfelt twist to this rescue. Arthur has adjusted well to his new California lifestyle, blending in seamlessly with the other Latour animals. Meanwhile, the Egan family is sending out a photo of Marty Jr., a picture the Latours plan to frame and hang on the family picture wall.

Pets of Military Personnel

Another consequence of the September 11th tragedy has been the activation and deployment of U.S. military forces overseas, including soldiers who happen to have pets at home. As these troops are being called up, those without immediate family are having to decide what to do with their pets.

A number of national humane societies, including The Humane Society of the United States (HSUS) and the American Humane Association (AHA) are urging military families to keep the pets at home and not relinquish them to local shelters. "If you're in the military, it's important to make prior arrangements for your pets in case you are deployed," says Nancy Peterson of HSUS. "When leaving your pet with family or friends, it's a good idea to create a foster care agreement (See HSUS Foster Care Agreement between Military Pet Owner and Caregiver in Resources.) Having a written agreement will help protect your pet and provide you with the security of knowing your chosen caretaker has the legal right to care for your pet in your absence."

Linda Pollack Mercer, DVM, president of the Feline Rescue Network, is organizing volunteer foster homes nationwide for "Operation Noble Foster." The program will care for the dogs, cats, and birds of military personnel who are deployed. "During the Desert Storm call up, many animal shelters and rescue groups reported a significant increase in animal turn-ins," says Mercer.

The events of September 11th are unprecedented. While most of these stories involving companion animals concluded on a positive note, what happened in New York City and in Washington D.C. serves as a powerful reminder of the importance of being prepared. For your own safety—and the safety of your pets.

Resources

Sample Will Pet Provision

[Article Number] A. As a matter of high priority and importance, I direct my Personal Representative to place any and all animals I may own at the time of my death with another individual or family (that is, in a private, noninstitutionalized setting) where such animals will be cared for in a manner that any responsible, devoted pet owner would afford to his or her pets. Prior to initiating such efforts to place my animals, I direct my Personal Representative to consult John Smith, DVM, currently at the Smallville Pet Hospital, or in the event of Dr. Smith being unavailable, a veterinarian chosen by my Personal Representative, to ensure that each animal is in generally good health and to alleviate suffering, if possible. Any animal(s) not generally in good health or who is suffering and whose care is beyond the capabilities of veterinary medicine, reasonably employed, to restore to generally good health or to alleviate suffering—shall be euthanized, cremated, and the ashes disposed of at the discretion of my Personal Representative. Any expenses incurred for the care (including the costs of veterinary services) placement, or transportation of my animals, or to otherwise effect the purpose of this Article___ up to the time of placement, shall be charged against the principal of my residuary estate. Decisions my Personal Representative makes under this Article___ shall be final. My intention is that my Personal Representative have the broadest possible discretion to carry out the purposes of this paragraph.

—From "Planning for Your Pet's Future Without You", The Humane Society of the United States

Sample Will Provision for Leaving Pets to an Animal Shelter

"I give all my [dogs, cats, and other animals] to the [Name of Shelter], presently located at [Address], with the following requests:

• that the shelter take possession of and care for all my animals and search for good homes for them;

• that until homes are found for my animals, the animals be placed in foster homes rather than cages at the shelter;

• that if it is necessary to keep some of the animals in cages while making arrangements to find permanent homes, in no event should any animal stay more than a total of two (2) weeks in a cage;

• that each animal should receive appropriate veterinary care, as needed;

• that after attempts have been made for three (3) months to place an animal, my personal representative [Name], presently residing at [Address], be contacted if it is not possible to place an animal so that my representative can assist with finding a home for the animal;

• that the shelter make every effort to assure that none of my animals are ever used for medical research or product testing under any circumstances;

• that, after placement, shelter staff make follow-up visits to assure that my animals are receiving proper care in their new homes.

If the [Name of Shelter] is in existence at the time of my death and is able to accept my animals, I give [$ Amount] to the shelter. If the shelter is unable to accept my animals, I give my animals and [$ Amount] to one of the charitable organizations as my Executor shall select, subject to the requests made above."

—From the Association of the Bar of the City of New York

Sample Veterinary Pet Care Contract

Mr. John Smith, desiring to provide quality medical care for his beloved cat, Homer, is entering into this agreement with Jane Brown, D.V.M. of Hillcrest Animal Hospital. The parties agree to the following terms:

1. Mr. Smith has paid Dr. Brown the amount of $5,000.

2. In return, Dr. Brown has agreed to provide complete veterinary care and services for Mr. Smith's cat, Homer. The time period for such care begins with the death of Mr. Smith and ends with the death of Homer.

3. Dr. Brown is entitled to administer care as she deems appropriate, but basic check-ups, vaccinations, and medications are expected, as needed.

4. Should Dr. Brown determine that Homer has a terminal condition, she has the right to withhold further treatment and opt for humane euthanasia. She is also asked to arrange for burial per Mr. Smith's instructions.

5. Should Dr. Brown retire from veterinary practice while Homer is still alive, she agrees to find another practitioner to carry out this agreement.

6. Any remaining funds from the original $5,000 after Homer's death is to be donated in the cat's name to the Plainfield Humane Society.

HSUS Foster Care Agreement Between Military Pet Owner and Caregiver

1. Owner hereby delivers to and deposits with the Caregiver said animal.

2. Upon the Owner's return from active duty, the Caregiver will return the animal to the Owner, which will be accomplished as soon as practical.

3. Due to the unknown duration of active duty, and the need of the Caregiver to know when the foster arrangements will be concluded, Owner agrees that the Caregiver will not be responsible for keeping the animal any longer than twelve (12) months from the date of this Agreement. Further if the Owner does not return within the twelve (12) month period, then Owner relinquishes any claim, right, title, or interest in said animal, and the said animal becomes the property of the Caregiver.

4. Owner may extend the twelve (12) month period stated above if the owner gives written notice to the Caregiver at least thirty (30) days before the end of the twelve month period that he or she wants to extend for up to an additional twelve (12) months.

5. Caregiver agrees not to alter in any way the appearance of the animal being fostered without written permission of the Owner. This includes declawing and cropping of ears or tails.

6. Caregiver agrees to provide adequate food, water, shelter and humane treatment for said animal at all times. Caregiver agrees to follow all oral and/or written instructions from the Owner.

7. If said animal dies or becomes accidentally injured, ill, or lost, Owner does not hold Caregiver responsible and releases the Caregiver from any claim arising from said injury. Owner will hold harmless and idemnify, and protect the Caregiver from any claim or suit filed by anyone as a result of such an incident.

8. The Caregiver reserves the right to seek veterinary care without approval by the Owner. Should medical care for the animal be warranted, the Owner authorizes up to $_____ to be provided to cover the cost for care. In addition, the Caregiver reserves the right to euthanize the animal should a veterinarian deem the animal's health to be so impaired that to sustain the animal would be inhumane.

CONTACTS

The following resources are for informational purposes only. This listing does not represent an endorsement by the authors or publisher.

ANIMAL SHELTER LONG-TERM CARE PROGRAMS

Marin Humane Society
171 Bel Marin Keys Blvd.
Navato, CA 94949
(415) 883-4621
www.marin-humane.org

Oregon Humane Society
1067 NE Columbia Blvd.
Portland, OR 97211
(503) 285-7722
www.oregonhumane.org

San Francisco SPCA Sido Service
2500 Sixteenth Street
San Francisco, CA 94103
(415) 554-3000
www.sfspca.org

Seattle Animal Control
2061 15th Ave. West
Seattle, WA 98119
(206) 386-4286
www.ci.seattle.wa.us/rca/animal

SPCA of Monterey County
P.O. Box 3058
Monterey, CA 93942
(877) 477-2262
www.spcamc.org

SPCA of Pinellas County
9099 130th Avenue North

Largo, FL 33773
(727) 581-3249
www.spcaofpinellas.org

SPCA of Texas
362 S. Industrial Blvd.
Dallas, TX 75207
(214) 651-9611
www.spca.org

PET RETIREMENT HOMES AND ANIMAL SANCTUARIES

Best Friends Animal Sanctuary
5001 Angel Canyon Rd.
Kanab, UT 84741
(435) 644-2001
www.bestfriends.org

Bide-A-Wee Golden Years Home
410 East 38th Street
New York, NY 10016
(212) 532-6395
www.bideawee.org

Bluebell Foundation for Cats
20982 Laguna Canyon Rd
Laguna Beach, CA 92651
(949) 494-1586

The Gabriel Foundation
P.O. Box 11477
Aspen, CO 81612
(877) 923-1009
www.thegabrielfoundation.org

Home for Life Animal
Sanctuary
P.O. Box 847
Stillwater, MN 55082
(800) 252-5918
www.homeforlife.org

Humane Society of Boulder Valley
2323 55th Street
Boulder, CO 80301
(303) 442-4030
www.boulderhumane.org

LaCrosse Avian Rescue
P.O. Box 1413
LaCrosse, WI 54602
(608) 787-0566
www.avianrescue.org/larra

Midwest Avian Adoption &
Rescue
P.O. Box 821
Stillwater, MN 55082
(651) 275-0568
www.maars.org

North Shore Animal League
25 Davis Ave.
Port Washington, NY 11050
(516) 883-7575
www.nsal.org

Progressive Animal Welfare
Society
P.O. Box 1037
Lynnwood, WA 98046
(425) 787-2500
www.paws.org

Silver Streak Kennel
129 Bourne Rd.

Morris, NY 13808
(607) 263-2007
www.dogretirement.com

Sylvester House
P.O. Box 896
Lompoc, CA 93438
(805) 735-6741

Wild Cat Ranch
137 Upper Sisterdale Rd.
Comfort, TX 78013
(830) 995-4689
www.wildcatranch.net

VETERINARY SCHOOL LONG-
TERM CARE PROGRAMS
Kansas State University
College of Veterinary Medicine
Office of Development
Manhattan, KS 66506
(785) 532-4833

Oklahoma State University
College of Veterinary Medicine
Director of Development
Stillwater, OK 74078
(405) 744-6728

Purdue University
School of Veterinary Medicine
Peace of Mind Program
West Lafayette, IN 47907
(765) 494-7608

Texas A&M University
College of Veterinary Medicine
Stevenson Companion Animal
Center
College Station, TX 77843
(979) 845-1188

References

Books

Condon, Gerald M. and Condon, Jeffrey L., *Beyond the Grave: The Right Way and the Wrong Way of Leaving Money to Your Children (and Others)*, Harper Business, 1995

Congalton, David, *Three Cats, Two Dogs, One Journey Through Multiple Pet Loss*, NewSage Press, 2000

Faler, Richard, *Pet Trust: A Last Will and Testament for You and Your Pet*, Beaver Pond Publishing, 1998

Randolph, Mary, *Dog Law: A Legal Guide for Dog Owners and Their Neighbors*, Nolo Press, 1997

Wilcox, Bonnie and Walkowicz, Chris, *Old Dogs, Old Friends*, Hungry Mind Books, 1991

Wise, Steven M., *Rattling the Cage: Toward Legal Rights for Animals*, Perseus Publishing, 2000

Articles

Arena, Salvatore, "Testament to Family: JFK Jr. Left Sis, Kids His Estate," *New York Daily News*, September 25, 1999

Berkman, Eric, "Estate Planning for Pets?" *Lawyers Weekly*, October 18, 1999

Beyer, Gerry W., "Pet Animals: What Happens When Their Humans Die?" *Santa Clara Law Review*, 2000, p. 40

Brock, Fred, "After the Pipe and Slippers Are Gone," *New York Times*, September 2, 2001

Brooks, Diane, "Couple Says Pets They Gave Away Were Sold for Slaughter," *Seattle Times*, July 1, 2001

Coeyman, Marjorie, "Finding Shelter," *Christian Science Monitor*, September 26, 2001

De Haven, Todd, "What Will Happen to Your Pets When You Die?" *Greeneville (TN) Sun*, August 14, 1999

Evarts, Eric, "Warm Heart, Cold Nose, Big Bucks!" *Christian Science Monitor*, August 17, 1998

Fitzpatrick, Edward, "Pet Trusts Let Owners Rest in Peace," *Albany Times-Union*, March 1, 1998

Heller, Bette, "Trusts for Pets," *The Colorado Lawyer*, March, 1997, p. 26

Helser, Linda, "Owners Are Making Provision in Their Wills for Animals' Care," *Arizona Republic*, May 13, 1998

Hubert, Cynthia, "Aid, Comfort Extended to Pets Near the N.Y. Attacks," *Sacramento Bee*, September 30, 2001

Krengel, Sharon, "Owners Should Address Pet's Welfare in Wills," *Detroit News*, February 23, 2000

MacNab, J.J., "In Dog We Trust—Not a Good Idea for Philanthropy," *Chronicle of Philanthropy*, June 28, 2001

May, Meredith, "Orphaned N.Y. Cat Finds Bay Area Home," *San Francisco Chronicle*, October 19, 2001

McGonagle, John J., "Planning for Your Cat's Care If You Are No Longer There," *Cats Magazine*, September 1992

Oliver, Judith, "Will of the People Saves Two Show Dogs," *Pittsburgh Post-Gazette*, January 23, 1994

Saltonstall, Dave, "Dog Friday, Cat Ruby Safe," *New York Daily News*, July 25, 1999

Schwartz, Barbara, "Estate Planning for Animals," *Trusts and Estates*, 1974, p. 376

Smith, Joan Lowell, "Plan for Possibility of Pet Outliving You," *Newark Star-Ledger*, August 5, 2001

Stone, Pamela, "Couple Will Let Their Luxury Home Go to the Dogs," *Dallas Morning News*, March 30, 1999

Taylor, Jennifer R., "A 'Pet' Project for State Legislatures: The Movement Towards Enforceable Pet Trusts in the Twenty-First Century," *Quinnipiac Probate Law Journal*, 1999, p. 13

Teichert, Nancy, "Families, Hospice Now Face Pets' Fate," *Sacramento Bee*, November 6, 2000

Triolo, Steve, "Cat Retirement Homes and Programs," *Cat Fancy*, July, 2001

Waldron, John F., "Attorneys See More Clients Including Provisions for Pets in Their Wills," *San Antonio Business Journal*, November 17, 2000

Walker, Joan Hustace, "When Rescue Hits Home," *Whole Cat Journal*, November, 2001

Ward, Drew, "Pet Owners' Wills Make Provisions for Fido and Fluff to Go to College," *Wall Street Journal*, June 10, 1996

INTERNET SOURCES

American Animal Hospital Association, "Pet Owner Statistics," www.aaha.org

American Pet Association, "Pet Statistics 1998," www.apapets.com

Beyer, Gerry W., "Estate Planning for Non-Human Family Members," www.professorbeyer.com

Green, Jorie, "Senior Pets Retire in Style," www.vetcentric.com

Haidar, Suhasini, "Stranded Pets Now Being Rescued," www.cnn.com

Humane Society of the United States, "Planning for Your Pet's Future Without You," www.hsus.org

Jensen, Alan, "Tax and Estate Planning Involving Pets: Stupid Pet Tricks for the IRS and FIDO," www.weiss-law.com

Palley, John B., "Think About Estate Planning for Pets," www.palley.com

Purina Pet Institute, "Helping Our Pet Companions Enjoy Their Golden Years," www.investor.cnet.com

Salzman, Marian, "Report on Pet Owner Buying Trends by Euro RSCG Worldwide," www.eurorscg.com

Shery, Beth G. "First Presidential Pets Were Birds," www.realmacaw.com

Shipley, Gerhard, "Pet Trusts: Providing for Pets," www.keln.org

Spadafori, Gina, "Estate Planning Should Include Provisions for Pets," www.vin.com/PetCare/Articles/PetConnection

Spadafori, Gina, "Gabriel Foundation Provides Safe Haven for Birds," www.vin.com/PetCare/Articles/PetConnection

Spadafori, Gina, "Who Will Help Your Pet If You Can't?" www.vin.com/PetCare/Articles/PetConnection

Sweat, Rebecca, "Birds of a Feather: Saving Unwanted Birds," www.petplace.com

Wahrhaftig, Matt, "Report of the Society for the Improvement of Conditions of Stray Animals," www.sicsa.org

Walker, Sherrie, "Homeless Pets—A National Shame," www.suite101.com

Wood, Keith A., "What Will Happen to Your Pets After You Are Gone?" www.petplacetoday.com

INDEX

ABOUT THE AUTHORS

David Congalton is an award-winning radio talk show host, author, and animal welfare advocate. His first book, *Three Cats, Two Dogs, One Journey Through Multiple Pet Loss* was published by NewSage Press in 2000. This book won the 2001 Merial Human-Animal Bond Award for Best Writing from the Dog Writers Association of America. Congalton hosts a popular radio talk show, which airs daily in Central California. He also writes for several national publications on veterinary health care and the human-animal bond.

Charlotte Alexander is a freelance writer, editor, and animal welfare advocate. She currently is serving her third term as president of the North County Humane Society in Atascadero, California. In 1998, Alexander was selected as Woman of the Year from her California State Senate District. Her feature articles appear monthly in the *San Luis Obispo County Journal*. Alexander has taught public relations and broadcast writing at the college level and is an award-winning publications, editing, marketing, and public relations specialist.

The authors, who have been married since 1989, share their Central Coast home with a menagerie of dogs and cats, all rescue animals. They can be reached through their website at www.AlexanderCongalton.com.

OTHER TITLES BY NEWSAGE PRESS

NewSage Press has published several titles related to animals. We hope these books will inspire humanity towards a more compassionate and respectful treatment of all living beings.

Three Cats, Two Dogs: One Journey Through Multiple Pet Loss
Award Winner, Merial Human-Animal Bond, Best Book
by David Congalton

Blessing the Bridge: What Animals Teach Us About Death, Dying, and Beyond
by Rita M. Reynolds

Food Pets Die For: Shocking Facts About Pet Food
by Ann N. Martin

Protect Your Pet: More Shocking Facts
by Ann N. Martin

Singing to the Sound: Visions of Nature, Animals & Spirit
by Brenda Peterson

Conversations with Animals: Cherished Messages and Memories as Told by an Animal Communicator
by Lydia Hiby with Bonnie Weintraub

Dancer on the Grass: True Stories About Horses and People
by Teresa Tsimmu Martino

The Wolf, the Woman, the Wilderness: A True Story of Returning Home
by Teresa Tsimmu Martino

Unforgettable Mutts: Pure of Heart Not of Breed
by Karen Derrico

Polar Dream: The First Solo Expedition by a Woman and Her Dog to the Magnetic North Pole
by Helen Thayer, Foreword by Sir Edmund Hillary *(available August 2002)*

NEWSAGE PRESS

For more information visit our website
www.newsagepress.com

or request a catalog from NewSage Press
PO Box 607, Troutdale, OR 97060-0607
Phone Toll Free 877-695-2211, Fax 503-695-5406
Email: info@newsagepress.com

Distributed to bookstores by Publishers Group West
800-788-3123